The Participatory Economy

*An Evolutionary Hypothesis and
a Strategy for Development*

The Participatory Economy

*An Evolutionary Hypothesis and
a Strategy for Development* ≺≺≺≺≺

Jaroslav Vanek

CORNELL UNIVERSITY PRESS / ITHACA AND LONDON

First published 1971 by Cornell University Press.
Published in the United Kingdom by
Cornell University Press Ltd.,
2–4 Brook Street, London W1Y 1AA.

International Standard Book Number 0-8014-0639-0
Library of Congress Catalog Card Number 77-148024

PRINTED IN THE UNITED STATES OF AMERICA
BY VAIL-BALLOU PRESS, INC.

To Josef, Francis,
Rosemarie, and . . .

Preface ≺≺≺≺≺≺≺≺≺≺≺≺≺≺

Most of my research over the past ten years has been directed toward the study, both theoretical and empirical, of an economy based on workers' participation in managing and in sharing the income of enterprises. This research led to the publication of *The General Theory of Labor-Managed Market Economies* (Ithaca, N.Y., 1970), which contains the rigorous and strictly economic results of my work. It does not, however, represent the totality of my thoughts on the subject.

Quite unavoidably, if one studies for many years what today seems to be a new major economic system, differing from both western capitalism and the Soviet-type command economy, one is led to entertain many questions going beyond the confines of economic analysis. Also quite unavoidably, one keeps trying to find answers to such questions. Unfortunately or fortunately, one's curiosity is not limited to one's professional field.

At the same time it is difficult to include, in a single volume, nonprofessional or general reflections with the so-called expert findings. Such a study would necessarily be too technical and too difficult for the general reader and at the same time might strike the professional economist as ballasted by too many broad reflections. Consequently, once I had decided to publish my general thoughts, I had to do so in a separate volume. Because the volume is primarily intended for the general audience, I have also attempted in its early chapters to summarize in a simple manner the essentials of the earlier study.

Besides economics, the subject matter of this book bears or at least borders on several fields that are not my own —history, sociology, political science, philosophy, and perhaps even psychology. This small volume ought therefore to be taken as a general essay and not as a scholarly product of any of the fields noted. My justification for having written the book is a deep conviction that the subject with which I deal is most important and timely, and that the key points made in it are true.

I should like to express my sincere thanks to Mrs. Florence Finch, secretary of the Program on Participation and Labor-Managed Systems at Cornell, for all her help in preparing the manuscript for publication.

J. V.

Ithaca, New York

Contents ≺≺≺≺≺≺≺≺≺≺≺≺≺≺

The Participatory Economy

An Evolutionary Hypothesis and
a Strategy for Development

1 ≺≺≺≺≺≺≺≺≺≺≺≺≺≺≺≺≺

Introduction

The quest of men to participate in the determination and decision-making of the activities in which they are personally and directly involved is one of the most important sociopolitical phenomena of our times. It is very likely to be the dominant force of social evolution in the last third of the twentieth century. We are witnessing this trend within and outside our country, in universities and enterprises, as well as in national, state, and local policy-making. The fact that perhaps the most pronounced and most articulate form of the participatory tendencies is to be found among the young suggests not only that these tendencies are here to stay but they will be with us in ever-increasing degree.

Given these facts, it is perfectly natural to inquire about the potential economic effects of participation. More specifically—what effects can management by employees be expected to have on an economy that adopts it as the basic *modus operandi* in all of its firms? Can such an economy be expected to produce as much from its national resources as a capitalist economy, or as a socialist centrally planned

economy? How will it perform in attaining full employment of the population? Will it tend to be inflationary or
not? Can it be expected to generate high levels of economic
growth, development, and expansion? These are only a few
questions among those that could be asked in the sphere of
economics.

But there are other much broader, and in some respects
more important questions. Perhaps the most significant is
whether a participatory economy will tend to produce a
more harmonious social environment or not. Is it likely to
alleviate frictions and antagonisms among social classes?
Can the international political situation be favorably affected by the development of participatory economies?

The first of the three major objectives of the present
study is an analysis of the participatory economy—we will
also refer to it as the *labor-managed market economy*—
with a view toward answering such economic and noneconomic questions as the ones raised above. In answering
the economic questions we survey the main theoretical
arguments for and against labor management and examine
the performance of the one significant labor-managed economy in the world, the economy of Yugoslavia.

While this entire book is an attempt to seek answers to
the broad noneconomic questions, the economic questions
are dealt with in the three subsequent chapters. The first
of these, Chapter 2, is devoted to the identification of what
we understand by the participatory, or labor-managed
economy. It is necessary to explain exactly, and in an operational manner, the meaning of labor management, before
any analysis of its behavior and performance can be undertaken. It is also necessary to point out the fundamental

differences between a participatory economy and the major existing models of organization—that is, the western-capitalist and Soviet-type command economies. The principal characteristics of the labor-managed economy once defined, we turn in Chapter 3 to the analysis of its potential—or theoretical—performance. In Chapter 4, finally, we examine the key data regarding the performance of the labor-managed economy of Yugoslavia.

Besides fulfilling a part of our first objective, Chapters 2–4 also constitute the necessary basis for the other two objectives. These are, first, the incorporation of the theory of a participatory economy into a broader, coherent theory of social, political, and economic evolution, and second, the examination of the participatory economy as a vehicle of economic development and over-all advancement for the poorer countries. Chapters 5–7 are devoted to the first of these objectives and Chapter 8 to the second.

The exposition of what constitutes our area of exploration follows a familiar method. First, in Chapter 5 we state the evolutionary theory in a general and abstract form, so as to give the reader an overall notion of the matter. The subsequent two chapters, on the other hand, constitute what we might call the "supporting material," that is, historical and other factual substantiation of the theory. (I prefer here the term "substantiation" rather than "proof" because there is no question of proving hypotheses in social science as broad as those we are concerned with.)

The essence of the theory of social evolution is transposed from general equilibrium analysis in economics—whereto, in turn, it was brought from physics—and claims that for a state of full equilibrium a set of equilibrium conditions (six in our case) must all be fulfilled simultaneously. Moreover, if some or all conditions are violated, then necessarily the social system will be in a state of flux—that is, will undergo continuous transformations—which will be governed by laws dependent, in part at least, on the specific nature of the disequilibrium.

It is the history of modern industrial societies which furnishes the supporting material for the theory of social evolution expounded here. In Chapter 6 we look at Western capitalism, as it evolved approximately from the time of the industrial revolution. In Chapter 7 we examine in the same context the evolution within the socialist bloc, beginning from the period of the Russian revolution. In neither case is it our objective to present a complete or coherent rein-terpretation of history; rather we aim to bring together our abstract theory with the key transformations which have led to the two major world systems of today. In both in-stances, the analysis is, by and large, carried out in two distinct steps. First, we attempt to characterize the state of disequilibrium as it could be found in the two major systems at various periods, including the present; and second, we attempt to interpret the major transformations from one state into another, relying, as much as possible, on the dy-namic mechanism of the evolutionary theory. Of course, the reader should not expect here an exact quantitative analysis as we know it from physics or theoretical eco-nomics, but rather an approximate and qualitative line of reasoning.

As a by-product on the plane of evolution of socio-economic and political thought, our theory also makes it possible in several instances to give a broader foundation to, or fit into a more general logically consistent pattern, certain major ideas which have stirred the public consciousness in recent years. Thus, for example, Galbraith's "new industrial state" with its emphasis on the management-controlled large corporation can be interpreted as an evolutionary substage of a more general trend.[1] Or Servan-Schreiber's thesis of technological "retardation" can be identified as a symptom of violation of an equilibrium condition, and thus as a force of socioeconomic transformation.[2]

Moreover, and perhaps more important, when extrapolated—or projected—into the future, the theory of social evolution suggested here lends support to the theories of "convergence" of world systems advanced in many quarters. In fact, in its application to the future, our theory itself becomes a theory of convergence. The principal purpose of the concluding chapter (Chapter 9) is precisely the substantiation of this claim. We attempt to put together in rough outline what we know about the present with the theory of evolution developed here in order to arrive at a set of "plausible expectations" for the future. In this sense, Chapter 9 also contributes to our second major objective of incorporating our theory into a broader context. It also derives, however, from our study of labor management as a vehicle of economic advancement for the less developed countries; that is, from what we have referred to before as the third and last major objective of the study.

[1] John Kenneth Galbraith, *The New Industrial State* (Boston, 1967).
[2] Jean-Jacques Servan-Schreiber, *The American Challenge* (New York, 1968).

Chapter 8 is devoted to that objective. In it we bring together the other elements of analysis of the labor-managed economy with the most important aspects of the problem of economic development. In doing this we try to show that labor management can be not only a viable but a highly desirable strategy for development.

2 ≺≺≺≺≺≺≺≺≺≺≺≺≺≺≺≺≺

Identifying
the Participatory Economy

We must start our discussion by explaining, far more carefully than we were able to do in the preceding chapter, what we understand by the participatory—or labor-managed—economy. The matter is not a simple one because any definition at this stage of history must be a judicial balancing of what we observe in the real world and what we can identify as the most desirable form of participatory economy on grounds of a priori scientific judgment. To say that the participatory economy is exactly the type of economy we find today in Yugoslavia would be as incorrect and one-sided as to say that labor management consists of a number of abstract principles unrelated to any real experience or actual performance.

Fortunately, there is another factor which will help us in seeking a definition. We do not have to identify the participatory economy down to the minutest detail, there being a very large number of characteristics which may be termed nonessential and which can be adjusted to particular situations or circumstances. For example, a number of minor characteristics of the participatory economy of Yugoslavia could certainly be omitted or replaced by others —indeed, this might be highly desirable—if a specific labor-managed economy were designed for, say, a country of Latin America or Africa. We thus have to concentrate here only on what we may term basic characteristics of a system of economic participation; the rest can be left for adaptation to specific conditions. In fact it is this adaptability that makes—or at least promises to make—the participatory economy universally appealing.

To use an analogy, we may liken the labor-managed economy—or for that matter, any economy—to a motor vehicle. If we want to become acquainted with the vehicle, we should learn principally about two things: one, what are the vehicle's main component parts, and two, what is its moving force? Accordingly, we will first introduce a set of defining characteristics of the labor-managed economy, and then explain what its principal moving force is— that is, the motivation on which economic actions within it are actually taken. Pushing the analogy a step further, we may also ask how the vehicle compares with other vehicles in respect to the main component parts. And going still another step, we may want to learn how the moving force—that is, the motor—compares with that of other vehicles. These other aspects of characterization by comparison will also concern us in this chapter.

The first of our five defining characteristics is quite obvious. The labor-managed or participatory economy is one based on, or composed of, firms controlled and managed by those working in them. This *participation in management* is by *all* and on the basis of equality, that is, on the principle of one-man one-vote.[1] It is to be carried out in the most efficient manner—in the majority of cases through elected representative bodies and officers: a workers' council, an executive board, and the director of the firm.

Clearly, the exact form of labor management that is most efficient can vary from enterprise to enterprise and from one labor-managed economy to another, and as such need not concern us here. It could not be overemphasized that the participation in control and management derives uniquely and unalterably from *active* participation in the enterprise. Participation in ownership in no way and under no circumstances entails the right to control and manage; whether active participants are also owners of the assets of the firm or whether they contribute to the formation of such assets through undistributed earnings, it is not these contributions but their active participation that entitles them to control and manage.

The second general characteristic is related to and, in a sense, derives from the first. It is *income sharing*. The participants of the labor-managed firm, after they have paid for all material and other costs of operation, share in the income of the enterprise. This sharing is to be equitable, equal for labor of equal intensity and quality, and governed by a democratically agreed-on income-distribution schedule assigning to each job its relative claim on total net income.

[1] Alternatively, in a more sophisticated and generally superior voting scheme where the voters are allowed to assign different weights to alternative issues simultaneously to be decided on, each voter is given the same number of points. This reflects the principle of equality of importance among members engaging in the democratic process of decision-making.

Of course, not all of net income needs to be distributed to individual participants; a collectively agreed-on share can be used for reserve funds, various types of collective consumption, or investment. In the last-mentioned instance, however, for reasons which will become apparent in the rest of this chapter and in the next, it may be preferable to recognize the contributions of savings to the firm's capital formation as individual claims of each participant, and express them in the form of fixed interest bearing financial obligations of the firm. Of course, recalling our first defining characteristic, such financial claims cannot under any circumstances carry a right to control or management of the firm.

These considerations of financing bring us to the third basic characteristic of participatory economies. The working community which has the exclusive right to control and manage the activities of the firm does not, as such, have the full ownership—in the traditional sense of the word "ownership"—of the capital assets which it uses. Perhaps the term *usufructus*, the right of enjoying the fruits of material goods, is a more appropriate one. The working community can enjoy the fruits of production in which the plant and equipment were used, but it must pay for this a contractual fee—or rental, or interest on the financial liability brought about by the purchases of such real assets. The community cannot destroy the real assets or sell them and distribute the proceeds as current income. In turn, the lenders of financial capital have no right of control whatsoever over the physical assets of the firm as long as the working community meets its debt-servicing obligations; the same holds for those who may lease physical assets to the firm, as long as the corresponding obligations of the labor-managed firm are met.

Whereas the first three defining characteristics pertain to individual firms, the remaining two bear on the relations among firms and, more generally, among all decision-making units of the participatory economy. The fourth characteristic is that the labor-managed economy must always be a *market economy*. This implies, among other things, that the economy is fully decentralized. All decision-making units, firms, households, associations, and the public sector decide freely and to their best advantage on actions they take, without direct interference from the outside. Economic planning and policy may be implemented through use of indirect policy instruments, discussion, improved information, or moral suasion, but never through a direct order to a firm or a group of firms. The economic relations among the above-mentioned decision-making units are settled through the conventional operation of markets, which is perfectly free whenever there are a sufficiently large number of buyers or sellers. Only in situations of monopolistic or monopsonistic tendencies can the public authorities interfere—and then only by fixing of maximum or minimum prices, or, preferably, by rendering the market structure more competitive, either through stimulation of entry or through opening up of the market to international competition. This ought not to be interpreted to mean that values determined by free market operation are desirable in any normative sense; a given society may prefer values different from those established by free competition (e.g., it may desire to make cigarettes prohibitively expensive) but if it does, it must reach its aims through legitimate tools of policy (a high tax on cigarettes or an import duty on imports of tobacco).

We come finally to the fifth basic characteristic. It bears on the human factor which in the participatory economy no longer is a mere factor of production but also—and perhaps primarily—the decision-making and thus creative and entrepreneurial factor. We may refer to the fifth characteristic as *freedom of employment*. It simply indicates that the individual is free to take, not to take, or to leave a particular job. At the same time, the labor-managed firms are free to hire or not to hire a particular man. However, the firms can, as a matter of their collective and democratic decision, limit in various ways their own capacity to expel a member of the community even where strictly economic considerations might call for doing so.

These considerations of freedom of employment—especially the one regarding the right to dismiss—lead us to the second part of identification of the participatory economy. What is the basic motivational force—or in the transposed sense suggested earlier, what is the motor—of the participatory firm and thus of the labor-managed economy as a whole?

In classical capitalism the moving force was the maximization of profit. In the Galbraithian new industrial state it is the self-interest of the upper management stratum of the large corporation, and in Soviet-type systems it is a combination of the fear of penalties attached to plan nonfulfillment and various types of bonuses extended to the plant manager.

In the participatory economy it is a combination of the interests of the members of the labor-managed firms as individuals on the one hand, and as a collective on the other. More specifically, and thinking first of the problem in pecuniary terms, the labor-managed firm's aim is the *maximization of income* for each of its members. Of course, this must be done in conformity with an income-distribution schedule reflecting the comparative shares belonging to each job agreed on democratically in advance; once the schedule is given, the highest income is attained for all participants at each level as soon as it is attained by any single participant.

This pecuniary objective of income maximization can be thought of as the crude form of the moving force of the labor-managed systems. It reflects an important part of the true motivation, and it lends itself to a simple formal analysis of the behavior of the labor-managed firms and of the labor-managed systems as a whole. It does not by any means contain the whole truth, however, and in many concrete situations will not even be seen as the principal objective by the participants of actual labor-managed firms.[2]

The true objective of the participatory firm is complex and multidimensional. If we insisted on reducing it to a single variable, we could not do otherwise than to say that

[2] In discussion with practical economists, enterprise directors, or workers in Yugoslavia, the income-maximizing motive will often not be recognized—or will be recognized only after some reflection —and other objectives, such as maximum growth, maximum surplus value, and maximum employment will be given. As an even more extreme point of view—one that certainly cannot be dismissed on a priori grounds—some will say that the objective of the participatory firm is simply what the majority of participants wants, there being no single identifiable motive.

the single variable is the degree of satisfaction of the individuals within the collective. Of course, monetary income may be an important ingredient of the satisfaction, especially in very poor environments, but it is definitely not the only one. The working collective can, for example, sacrifice some money income in exchange for additional leisure time, lesser intensity of work, better human relations —or even a kinder managing director. If this is so, all the alternatives mentioned must be considered as a part of the participatory firm's objective and thus as a component of the moving force of the labor-managed economy. In fact, the broader interpretation of the motivation base can include even objectives which normally would not be included under the heading of "self-interest," such as giving employment to others in the community, preventing unfavorable external effects of production such as air or water pollution, and many others.

For purposes of the evaluation of the functioning and performance of the participatory economy which we want to carry out in the next chapter, it will be useful to retain the distinction between the two levels of understanding of motivation in the participatory economy. We may refer to the crudely functioning income-maximizing objective as the *narrow motivation principle* and to the other, truer objective—which embraces a multiplicity of particular objectives—as the *broad motivation principle*.

Let us now leave the characterization through detailed description and turn to a characterization through comparison with the major economic systems as we find them in the world today. In what respects is the labor-managed economy similar to the capitalist systems of Western Europe and the United States and to Soviet-type command economies, and in what respects is it different? The emphasis here is on *distinction* or *differentiation,* and not on comparison of efficiency or desirability. The latter subject will be taken up in Chapter 3.

The key point that I would like to make is that some of the conventional ways of categorizing economic systems are not quite appropriate if we want to bring out the main distinguishing characteristics of labor-managed economies. More specifically, I submit that the principal distinguishing characteristic—we may refer to it henceforth as the *first-order distinction*—is one that separates the labor-managed economies from *both* of the two major world systems, which, under that categorization, belong to the same group. It is only the more conventional, and for our purposes *second-order distinction,* between capitalism and socialism, that allows us to draw the line between the two major world systems.

The first-order distinction hinges on who controls and manages the firm. Is it capital—that is, the owners of capital—or is it the working community? In the case of both conventional capitalism and Soviet-type socialism it is the former; in the case of the participatory economies it is the latter; and this is what we have referred to above as the first-order distinction. The second-order distinction, cutting across both categories just mentioned (i.e., the capital-controlled and the participatory) hinges on who actually owns the capital. In the capitalist alternative ownership is private; in the Soviet-type alternative ownership is by the state. Similarly, participatory economic systems can be based on private or social ownership, even if at present there are no real examples of the former alternative.

That what we have termed the first-order distinction is

the more important can be made more evident through an analogy. In the political context—going back two hundred years into American history—it is comparable to the political distinction between the colonial and postcolonial rule. In the former instance, as in western capitalism or in Soviet socialism, those who control and manage are *exterior* to the community or society controlled; in the latter case those who control—or govern—and those who are controlled— or governed—are one and the same community. Following this line of reasoning, our second-order distinction is comparable to the distinction between the colonial power in London emanating from the king (or queen) and emanating from the parliament. And this, from the point of view of the colonial Americans is a second-order—i.e., secondary —distinction indeed.

To push our analogy between political and economic realms a step further and conclude that the participatory alternative is humanly superior to the other alternatives might be deemed a value judgment. Nonetheless, I am confident that most of those who have experienced self-determination and democracy (whether political or economic) would concur. Regarding the strictly economic merits of the two major alternatives, we must, of course, defer judgment until the following two chapters.

We may now bring to a conclusion our definitional survey by saying a few words about the motivational base of the participatory economy—or, as we earlier termed it, the motor of the system (or vehicle in our metaphor). In the context of organized production in an enterprise two important questions can be asked about motivation. First, is it genuine or imposed, and second, is it shared by all or only some members of the working community? By genuine, I understand motivation which emanates from the natural inclinations and desires of an individual in a given environment; by contrast, an imposed motivation is one based on an instruction from an external controlling agent. Thus, for example, the motivation of a caretaker of a latifundium based on the absentee landlord's instruction to maximize profit, or the motivation of most soldiers going to battle, can be termed imposed. It is imposed because it is in conflict with the natural inclinations of the men concerned, and sustained only by the possibility of breach of contract or loss of a job. On the other hand, motivation of the "classical" capitalist-entrepreneur, that of a self-employed farmer, or of the community forming a labor-managed firm should be seen as genuine, because it is based on the natural inclinations of those concerned.

Whereas everybody employed must have at least the imposed motivation, what we have termed the genuine motivation is allowed by traditional economic systems to only some, often a small minority. By contrast, in the participatory economy, genuine motivation becomes the necessary rule for all of the working population, a situation inconceivable in any other industrial society.

Of course, an imposed motivation can be so designed, through bonus schemes and the like, as to approximate, for the managers of an enterprise at least, genuine motivation. Such schemes must, however, remain inferior to genuine motivation because the bonuses never exhaust the real income or output stimulated by them, because they hardly ever reach all of the workers and employees, and because a man-designed scheme can never be as comprehensive and perfect as something that is inherent in the natural state. To be more specific through an example with respect to the last three arguments, even with the possibility of a piece-work remuneration (that is, an artificial motivational scheme) it still will be possible to cheat on the quality of the product. In the case of a participatory firm (with genuine motivation) the man who would cheat on quality would know not only that the earnings or the goodwill of the firm, or both, would be impaired, but also that he might have to face the contempt of his fellow workers.

We have now seen what the participatory economy consists of and how it compares in several major respects with other economic systems. Only one major question remains to be answered if we want to obtain a clear picture of the participatory economy as a real phenomenon. The question is: How does one arrive at such an economy in the real world, a world adhering almost without exception to other forms of economic organization?

Clearly, one way to attain labor management is from a Soviet-type centralized economic system—as Yugoslavia did, and as Czechoslovakia in 1968 and perhaps other countries in Eastern Europe hoped to do. Another way is from a western-type economic organization as we find it in the noncommunist world. The latter evolution has never yet actually occurred in full, but partial developments in that direction, and the potential for a full adoption of a labor-managed system, exist not only in the less-developed parts of the noncommunist world but even in some advanced countries.

The transition from a Soviet-type command economy—we may refer to it as *transition from the left*—is very difficult politically. It may be achievable only as a by-product of violent political forces—as witnessed by Yugoslavia's bitter rupture with the Soviet Union in 1949. The opposing forces may be so violent, as witnessed by events in Czechoslovakia in 1968, as to suppress an incipient reform. On the other hand, institutionally and administratively, the transition is quite easy, as it involves, unquestionably, a considerable simplification of procedures—abolition of directive planning and its replacement by decentralization, far greater reliance on market forces, and indicative planning.

Regarding the *transition from the right*, that is, from and within a western-type market economy, matters seem to be just the other way around. The political or legal obstacles in most situations will not be insurmountable, especially if one does not insist on adopting a socialist variant of the participatory economy. The real difficulties and problems to be solved normally will be found in creating appropriate institutions and putting them to work. It may also be very difficult—in the short run at least—to overcome popular conservatism and resistance to innovation among those who think that they are favored by the established order.

Clearly, a good deal of educational work has to be done. Even the blue-collar workers and lower-echelon administration and technical staff who are bound to gain significantly from participation are likely at first to doubt the merits of the innovation—for the simple reason that they have never experienced it in practice.

As I have discussed in much more detail elsewhere, even more important than promotion and information is the creation of a proper environment, conducive to the formation and growth of labor-managed firms as defined earlier in this chapter.[3] Such an environment normally does not exist in western economies, whether developed or underdeveloped. Its main aspect is the possibility of funding new firms or expansions entirely through external financing, without sacrificing the independence of self-control required by labor management. Otherwise, if the labor-managed firms were primarily to rely on the personal funds of the founders, or on accumulation through current operation, the danger would always persist that the firm would degenerate into a traditional partnership with first- and second-class members. The owner-workers then might usurp the rights of self-management, and in extreme cases give up work altogether. Moreover, self-financing would be as liable to lead to inefficient allocation of scarce capital resources throughout the economy as in modern capitalist systems. Once again, it can scarcely be overemphasized that in a participatory economy the participation is by virtue of work, and is not related to the ownership of capital.

[3] *The General Theory of Labor-Managed Market Economies* (Ithaca, N.Y., 1970), Chapter 15. Normally, this will call for the formation of an institution—I have called it the National Labor Management Agency—capable of financing the participatory sector, and collecting and further reinvesting the returns from such loans. The agency can also serve as a powerful instrument of national planning, especially in the less-developed countries.

3 ‹‹‹‹‹‹‹‹‹‹‹‹‹‹‹‹‹‹‹‹

How Well Can the Participatory Economy Be Expected to Operate?

In the preceding chapter I have defined the participatory economy by giving its principal characteristics, and by distinguishing it from other economic systems. The next logical step is to take a look at how well the participatory economy can be expected to operate. There are two major possible approaches to the matter: theoretical and empirical. In this chapter we will use the first approach. In the subsequent chapter we will use the second, and attempt to answer the question insofar as possible by studying the actual performance of the Yugoslav economy.

Using the image of a vehicle as we did in the preceding chapter—or to be more specific, a bus—it is possible to ask a number of questions about the efficiency or degree of perfection of its operation. For example, how much transportation service does the bus provide per unit of fuel, labor, or capital invested? What is its maximum speed? Are seats in the front of the bus as comfortable as those in the back. Similarly, economists attempting to evaluate the performance of a given economic system will try to answer comparable questions: How close does the system come to the producible maximum consistent with resources? How fast can it grow—that is, expand its productive resources? How desirable is the income distribution to which it leads?

In this chapter we will ask about a dozen fundamental questions of this type about the participatory economy and attempt to answer them in a manner intelligible to the general reader. (At times, this will mean simply stating the conclusions of arguments presented in full in my earlier, more technical work on the participatory economy,[1] or providing only partial evidence.) Our answers will allow us to make a summary evalutation of the participatory system at the end of the chapter. Both in the individual arguments and in the overall conclusion, we will try to evaluate the participatory economy in two ways—on its own, that is, against an absolute standard of perfection, and in comparison with other economies, especially those found in the majority of countries in the western world.

The first question is about the attainment of a producible maximum. Economists tend to be a stubborn breed with a predilection for the perfection of markets, that is, perfect competition with a large number of buyers and sellers. Although such markets are almost nonexistent, economists nonetheless like to ask how well an economy would function if markets actually were perfect. The procedure is justifiable for two reasons. Even if we do not have perfect markets in actuality, the analysis of the perfect case tells us something about the upper limit of an imperfect system. Second, the perfect case usually provides the economist

[1] *The General Theory of Labor-Managed Market Economies* (Ithaca, N.Y., 1970).

with a convenient point of departure for his excursions, inept and incomplete as they often are, into the real world of imperfection.

For the perfect world, where, besides having perfect market conditions, all firms have complete access to the same technological information, and where drastic changes of conditions do not occur frequently, it can be shown that the participatory economy will produce the same optimal level of national product as the ideal competitive capitalist solution. Implicit in this conclusion is the postulate that labor is of the same constant quality in both systems, acting exclusively as a factor of production. For the participatory economy especially, this assumption is an oversimplification that will have to be eliminated later in our appraisal.

Starting from this ideal—or perfect—situation we can now move in the direction of reality, that is, in the direction of the imperfections that arise in actual economies. We can proceed via two different itineraries. One derives from the fact that in reality the economic environment changes and the economy must adjust to such changes. Hardly ever is it given the time to make a full adjustment, because before it can do so other changes in the environment occur. The other major line of argument that we must explore stems from the fact that most markets in reality are not perfect; in most instances we have only a small number of sellers, each of whom can exercise some degree of control over price and demand.

Before going into some of the more detailed arguments it will be useful to review the main conclusions regarding our two "approaches to the real world." Obviously, both imperfections tend to reduce national product from what it might be under the ideal conditions. As far as we can ascertain, these comparative losses of efficiency are neither negligible nor enormous in either the participatory or the western market economy. The comparative losses due to imperfections in adjustment of the economy to a changing environment, however, can on the whole be expected to be more serious in the participatory economy than in the western market economy. Just the reverse can be expected to be the case with respect to the inefficiencies resulting from market imperfections. Specifically, there is every reason to believe that market structures under labor management would be comparatively more competitive than in western market systems. Especially if one considers the damaging side effects of monopolistic forces, this edge of the participatory solution appears to be of considerable significance.

Let us now have a closer look at the problem of adjustment. One possible change in economic environment might occur when demand shifts from one product to another—when, for example, demand for television sets increases and that for radios diminishes. Obviously, it will take time for the adjustment to the change by producers to be made, and during that period some losses in national product will occur. These losses will be comparatively unimportant in both economies if the adjustment can be accomplished mostly within firms, as would normally be the case for our example: the same producers can shift from radios to television sets. The losses will be more sizable if resources—that is, labor and capital—must be shifted from one industry to another, as would be the case between radios and automobiles. While more significant in both systems, the losses will be comparatively greater—the adjustment being slower—in the participatory economy.

Turning now to the question of market concentration and monopolistic tendencies, we may say that in this context the deviation from the optimum in the participatory economy will generally not be considerable. It will certainly be less than in western capitalist market structures. Several arguments can be offered to substantiate this proposition. First, on strictly psychological and sociological grounds, in self-governing bodies which participate in collective income, there will be a natural tendency to break into the smallest possible operational units (collectives) consistent with economic efficiency. The simple reason for this is the natural desire not to have men functionally remote from one's position participate in decisions and income. Traditional and modern capitalist firms have, by contrast, the well-known tendency to grow without bounds, the interests of the majority of employees being neglected. Very often the capitalist firms will tend to grow even well beyond a size that would be warranted on grounds of efficient operation.

Another argument is more economic and its full development would call for an undue amount of technical analysis; its common sense can be explained, however, without much difficulty. Suppose that a labor-managed firm operates at a level or scale of operation which permits it to be efficient and competitive with other firms in its industry. At that level of operation each worker makes a given income. If now the firm were to double its output—without affecting price significantly—the income per laborer would by and large remain unchanged assuming that the internal efficiency of the firm were not affected. The conclusion is that under the assumed conditions (which, incidentally, are often encountered in reality) there would be no special desire on the part of the firm to grow because such growth would not improve the income of each worker. And consequently, from this point of view at least, there would be only a slight tendency within the industry to reduce competition—that is, lower the number of firms—once each firm attained its efficient scale of operation. By contrast, under capitalist conditions, doubling of output in our above example would have doubled profits, and this indeed would have served as a powerful incentive to growth and, in many cases, to an eventual complete elimination of competition.

Still another among the several arguments regarding the degree of competition is related to questions of product differentiation, sales promotion, and advertising. Because it concerns such a large number of markets in the real world and also for other reasons, to which we will turn presently, it is probably the most important argument in this general case. The participatory firm differentiating and promoting its product will, as can be shown,[2] in the overwhelming majority of cases engage in less promotional activity and operate at a lower level of output than a comparable capitalist firm. This leads to the conclusion that other things being equal, differentiated oligopolies (e.g., soft drinks, tooth paste, cigarettes, automobiles, and just about all modern final manufactured goods) under labor management will be much more competitive than capitalist

[2] This slightly involved technical argument is developed in *The General Theory of Labor-Managed Market Economies*, Chapter 6, section 7.

oligopolies as we know them in the western world. Moreover, and perhaps more important, the participatory alternative will advertise and promote less and thus utilize national resources more efficiently. Especially if we realize that the participatory firm will tend to omit some of the most aggressive forms of promotional activity, and if we recall of what low taste and quality such activity often is and what effects it may have on the minds, outlooks, and values of the public, the comparative advantages of labor management, on this account only, emerge as quite considerable.[3]

To sum up the arguments on competitiveness and market structure: we can say, without exaggeration, that the participatory economy naturally tends to embody the principle of "live and let live" much more than other market economies known to us today. There is far less urge to eliminate one's rival from the market. And this, let it be noted, carries within itself no implication of lesser efficiency. On the contrary, there is every reason to believe that oligopolies will on the whole be more efficient under labor management than under capitalism.

Even more obvious—not calling for any refined economics—is the related fact that in the participatory regime, by and large, there is no place for the labor-versus-management conflict. In consequence, the costs to society and to individual firms of strikes and other types of overt economic warfare are eliminated and the moral and mental costs of animosity, anger, and hatred are reduced.

Although this goes beyond the confines of economics—

[3] Cf. Lewis Mumford, *The Myth of the Machine* (New York, 1970).

and we will return to the subject in the noneconomic context in some of the later chapters—it may be pointed out even here that both of the arguments just made are bound to have far-reaching salutary effects on individuals and society. Both the "live and let live" forces of participation and the elimination of the major source of conflict in enterprises will necessarily be reflected in human attitudes and human relations throughout and even outside of the economic world, because the men acting in the economic, social, intellectual, family, or religious worlds will by and large carry the same habits, prejudices, experiences, and attitudes from one world to another.

We may now return to less abstract considerations, and examine the participatory economy from the point of view of what is usually referred to as macro-economics. In this field we ask questions about the over-all—or global—performance of an economic system. For example, does it guarantee full employment, or is it likely to lead to significant fluctuations in income or prices, or is it likely to generate inflationary forces?

Regarding the first question, the answer is that the participatory economy effectively does guarantee full employment. It does so in the sense that the economy normally will operate at, or very near, full employment, and if, as a result of some drastic disturbance, unemployment were to arise, there are forces inherent in the system that will tend to restore full employment. In this respect, the participatory economy has a definite edge over capitalist economies as we know them in the western world.

A similar advantage, absolute with respect to an absolute standard and relative with respect to other market systems, is that the participatory economy is far less likely to undergo cyclical depressions than are western market economies, and if such cycles were to occur they would be much less important.

By contrast, and deriving from the same forces, there is more likelihood in the participatory economy to encounter variations, both up and down, in the general price level. But by no means can this disadvantage be so serious as to offset the advantages of lesser or no fluctuations in real income, national product, and employment. No one will doubt that five per cent of the labor force thrown out of work is incommeasurably worse than a five per cent change in prices.

When it comes to long-range stability of prices, that is, the likelihood of secular inflationary pressures, the labor-managed economy again promises to lead to satisfactory solutions. With no union power to fix wage rates, and a natural tendency of participatory firms to hold employment, prices can move down as easily as they can move up.

This, over long periods, can add up to over-all secular price stability if monetary policy is not inflationary. By contrast, in the capitalist economy, where wages and prices are reduced far less willingly than they are increased, secular inflation is a virtual necessity in any economy committed to a full employment policy.

Thus far we have considered the principal aspects of the performance of the labor-managed economy in what we may refer to as its simplified or dehumanized form. Perhaps the second adjective is more descriptive of what we mean. All the results obtained up to this point are inherent in the participatory market economy merely on the assumption that the enterprises maximize income per man, each worker supplying work of equal and constant quality. This assumption is incomplete, and may be termed "dehumanized" because it neglects several key facts about the nature of the participatory economy. The most important among these are: (1) in each firm men of many different skills are brought together to cooperate, and this raises, among others, problems of income distribution; (2) besides being workers in their firms, the participants also share in the responsibility of management, which involves a good deal more than decisions to maximize income per man; (3) the quality of work is not, in fact, a constant for each man, and the process of participation in decision-making coupled with income-sharing tends to influence the quality, intensity and duration of work of each member of the enterprise.

Without going into the technical aspects of the question, it can be said that remuneration and income distribution among different job categories in the labor-managed firm will be influenced by two major sets of forces (1) market forces and (2) the collective expression of the will and distributional attitudes of the working community. Market forces, and, more specifically, competition among firms (both existing and potential entrants into an industry) and individuals will guarantee that there would not be in the economy major differences in remuneration for identical jobs performed with comparable intensity of work. On the other hand, the participatory decision-making process is bound to lead to income-distribution patterns within the enterprise reflecting the will of the collective; and this can be expected to lead to income-distribution patterns somewhat more equal than would result from market forces only.

The relation between participation in decisions and income on the one hand and the quality and intensity of work in the participatory firm on the other brings out what is probably the single greatest strength of the system under study. The labor-managed firm is without doubt best suited to generate optimal incentives to work—best suited, that is, for the members of the collective to find the optimal level of work effort in relation to the income of the firm generated by the effort, and in relation to other possible objectives of the firm. This question of incentives is so important in comparison with some other questions of productive efficiency—such as those discussed earlier in the context of what we have termed the "dehumanized" model—because the variable factor on which incentives act, that is, the degree of effort, can vary enormously. In the context of any real situation, it can vary incommensurately more than the degree of attainment of a producible maximum (see our first question discussed in this chapter) in the "dehumanized" model.

To substantiate this, let us ask what are the "reasonable" limits of variation in effort of a worker or of a working collective as reflected by the value of output of the firm. We can distinguish three attributes, or aspects, of what we call effort: duration of work, intensity of work, and quality of work. If we suppose that a reasonable range of variation of each attribute is between 100 and 200 per cent—which hardly anybody with real experience can contest—then the aggregate reasonable range for effort taken as a whole may be as high as between 100 and 800 (i.e., $2 \times 2 \times 2 \times 100$) per cent. And, accordingly, the reasonable range of value of product of a given firm will be of similar magnitude. Compared with this, the ranges of variation of possible performance imputable to other factors discussed earlier in this chapter appear as very small, if not negligible.

In developing countries, moreover, where often the constraining factors on the degree of effort are malnutrition and other symptoms of extreme poverty, the variation in effort connected with incentives may be even greater in the long run. Higher incomes engender better living conditions and these in turn engender greater strength and vitality and further ability to respond to incentives. Such a beneficial progression may never even get off the ground under capitalist regimes or under Soviet-type central planning, and thus the progress of the poor countries may be slowed down considerably.

Although Chapter 8 is devoted to labor management as a strategy for the economic development of the less-developed countries, a few remarks on the subject are called for here. First, it ought to be noted that an important bottleneck to development is often a lack of entrepreneurial and technical ability. In most developing countries such deficiencies are being overcome, if it is at all possible to do so, at high social costs. Of students sent to industrialized countries, a large proportion never return home, and the fact that preferential treatment must be given to entrepreneurs and developers of industry often leads to unjust distortions in distribution of income and wealth. The economies often can only hope that industries will develop in the direction most profitable for the country; often the only way in which a country can influence the structure and rate of development is by letting the public sector play the role of the entrepreneur, that is, by state ownership and management of firms.

The participatory economy offers definite advantages in

most of these respects. Not only can a national labor-management agency—in a mixed or fully participatory economy—plan development of skills and allocate such skills in directions most desirable to the economy, but it can finance industrial development without offering unjustifiable gains of wealth to a very few persons. It can do this without at the same time acquiring excessive power of control, since that power rests in the hands of the participants of individual firms. An important fact is that labor-managed firms will themselves engage in training and educating their members in far greater degree than other firms because such training constitutes (in contrast with capitalist firms) a part of the real income of the decision-makers.

In addition, as I have explained in my other study on this subject, the growth potential of the participatory economy as reflected in its capability to accumulate capital can be enormous, near or above the highest in the world today.[4] Because most capital accumulation in the less-developed countries is bound to come from social—or collective—sources to begin with, it is only natural that the income from such resources, paid by the labor-managed firms for their use, should be reinvested into further accumulation. In this way as much as 20 to 30 per cent of the (net) national product can be mobilized for investment in the long run, without anyone feeling the burden of such national savings. Of course, private savings of individuals can then be added on top of such high percentages to lead to savings rates unsurpassed in history.

To sum up, in the context of economic growth and development the participatory alternative permits handling many basic difficulties of developing countries. The three

[4] *General Theory of Labor-Managed Market Economies.*

advantages that I consider most important are (1) the economy's capability to mobilize human and capital resources, (2) an inherent institutional structure that lends itself well to over-all direction toward socially desirable objectives, and (3) its intrinsic tendency to preserve decentralized decision-making and avoid excessive administrative concentration of economic power. Of course, the third point also has very important implications in the political sphere for the preservation of political rights and independence.

Before concluding this chapter we ought to return from the context of economic development to that of general economics. The day-to-day and month-to-month process of participation in management and income by all members of the enterprise will unavoidably have a very large number of effects besides those that we have spoken of thus far. Also unavoidably, some will be positive and some negative; on balance, however, there can be no doubt that the democratization and humanization inherent in labor management will lead to positive results, and that these will be the more important the longer the economy is permitted to operate under the participatory regime, and the longer the exposure to it by the workers and the employees.

It would be impossible to list all the special effects—or what we may refer to as the special dimensions—of labor management, nor can we present a complete discussion of any single one of them. Nonetheless, we may attempt a brief account of some of the more important of these effects.[5]

[5] See also *The General Theory of Labor-Managed Market Economies*, Chapters 13 and 14.

We may start at random, selecting an argument of direct relevance to western industrial societies. It has to do with so-called external diseconomies, such as air or water pollution. The managers of labor-managed firms—that is, workers and employees—who live in the vicinity of their air- or water-polluting plants, are more likely to take care of, or reduce the undesirable external effects, even at a cost, than capitalist owners who may live thousands of miles away or may never have seen the businesses they own.

Another favorable point is that some laborer-managers may decide to take out some of their incomes in kind, say, in the form of a less strenuous or more hygienic job, where the principle of pecuniary profit maximization in the capitalist firm would not permit such a job improvement. A naïve person may object that this will make the participatory economy produce less real output than the capitalist; but it must be remembered that the building of the pyramids did not maximize social welfare, even if it may have maximized physical output.

For similar reasons, the participatory firm will be more likely to support education, training, and retraining of its members, when a strict profit motive might not suffice to do so. This phenomenon, actually verifiable in Yugoslavia, is of considerable importance for labor force development in the less-advanced countries.

Being much more closely related and exposed to local living conditions in the village, town, or borough, the worker-managers of the participatory firms are in a much better position to cope with social ills than are capitalist managers. The latter, who either have no direct exposure to such ills or are expected to maximize returns for the owners, cannot use the weight and resources of their positions.

Still another argument bears on collective consumption of various kinds by the membership of the participatory firm. In many instances, again most frequently in poorer countries, the community of the labor-managed firm may be the only group powerful enough, financially and organizationally, to initiate and carry out projects for collective consumption, such as housing projects, recreation facilities, and even school facilities. While it is true that other—that is, nonparticipatory—firms can do likewise, a strong case can be made to the effect that the participatory ones will be more apt and willing to assume such functions.

This sketch of some of the more important positive factors ought to be complemented by arguments of comparable weight that are negative or unfavorable to labor management. In my opinion, there are only two such arguments —and it is disputable whether even these are actually unfavorable. First, it can be argued that democratic processes of decision-making are often slower, more roundabout, and more friction-generating than dictatorial or administrative fiat decisions, and this may have unsalutary effects on the economic performance of the enterprise. While there is a good deal of truth in this notion, it also must be recognized that as in political democracy, all is a matter of degree of participation, and the proper degree can itself be sought through democratic procedures. Just as in the political sphere it would be highly inefficient to have a full participation on every small decision, it would be equally inefficient—or at least extremely risky—democratically to delegate full powers in all matters to a director of the firm (or, for that matter, to the president of a country) for twenty years. But the democratic process itself is in a position to strike the proper balance between such extremes. And the balance it strikes, after all, should be efficient in the sense that it is favored by the majority, even if it may imply a slightly lower output and income than might be reached otherwise. The well-being, collective and individual, of the working community is at least as much a positive good as the last five dollars earned or unearned. Also, it may be expected that the democratic decision-making process can be made both more speedy and more efficient, in the sense of leading to results superior to those obtainable by simple majority rule.

The second argument, only a part of which is unfavorable to the participatory solution, is related to the question of inventive and innovative activity. It cannot be denied that with smaller size and a lesser push toward growth in the participatory firm, there will be less possibility to finance *major* invention, innovation and product development by such firms, as compared to their capitalist counterparts. Of course, a counterargument could be given to the effect that innovation and invention can be assumed by independent labor-managed research firms fully devoted to such activity. But the real counterbalancing argument is that in the context of *minor* inventive and innovative activity, the participatory firm has a distinct advantage. Not only are the workers directly concerned to put into practice improvements they have thought of because they realize the direct benefits that this offers them, but the partici-

patory regime also provides them with appropriate channels of communication, through their elected representatives or otherwise, to have their ideas studied and adopted.

To sum up this chapter, it can be said that under the
scrutiny of economic theory the participatory economy
appears in a very favorable light, both in comparison to an
absolute standard of efficiency and in comparison with
other economic systems. In the context of absolute evaluation, it will tend to produce solutions at or very near the
conceivable maximum and can reach very high rates of
growth and development.

Comparatively—leaving aside the Soviet-type model as
a basically inefficient one (except perhaps when it comes to
income distribution)—there is every reason to believe that
the participatory economy is, all things considered, superior
to western capitalist economies. In the sphere of how well
it allocates resources in production, it has both advantages
and disadvantages compared to the western market alternative. It has a definite advantage in generating full employment, long-range price stability, and growth. A similar
comparative advantage, quite considerable in terms of its
quantitative implications, must be assigned to the labor-
managed solution in the context of what we may term its
"special dimensions," that is, dimensions largely absent
from economic systems where the role of labor is exclusively that of a factor of production. The empirical evidence that is available, as we shall see in Chapter 4, does
not contradict these findings.

4 ≺≺≺≺≺≺≺≺≺≺≺≺≺≺≺≺≺

The Participatory Economy of Yugoslavia and Its Over-all Performance

Fortunately, we do not have to rely entirely on the theoretical results presented in the preceding chapter when evaluating the performance of the labor-managed economy. In Yugoslavia a system in its essential characteristics very near to or identical with our definition of labor management —most often referred to by economists as workers' management—has been in operation since the early 1950's. We can thus use the Yugoslav experience in verifying some of the theoretical findings of the preceding chapter. We will first describe briefly the economy of Yugoslavia and then evaluate its performance. Of course, in the latter task we will be able to present to the reader only the most important and most general information. As in the preceding chapter, we are concerned with both an absolute evaluation and one in comparison with other types of economies.

Legislation instituting labor management was passed in Yugoslavia in 1951, and the economy made a rapid transition to that system. By 1953 workers' participation in management through elected workers' councils and participation in the income of enterprises was the basic operating principle in by far the larger portion of nonagricultural production. Even in agriculture, most of the larger producing units were run on the participatory principle. Henceforth, the government of Yugoslavia could influence the course and structure of the economy only through indirect instruments of economic policy, very much as is the case in western economies.

More specifically, a firm in Yugoslavia can be created by initiative of either the government, a local authority (commune), a group of individuals, or another existing firm. Once created—buildings built and machines installed —the firm assumes life of its own. Internally and in its relations with the outside it then depends entirely on the decisions of the working community, subject only to general legal forms and regulations, applicable to all firms in the economy. The principal elected decision-making body is the workers' council: the council deliberates and decides on major matters concerning the policy of the enterprise and elects the executive council. The most important decisions, affecting the enterprise in a fundamental manner over a long period of time, will normally be discussed and passed by the entire collective. Among these belong the determination of the income-distribution schedule and other basic statutes of the enterprise, major acquisitions or sales of physical plant and equipment, formation of a new firm, and the appointment or vote of confidence in the director.

The director of the enterprise is normally found through a public competition and approved by the working community; an endorsement by the commune or other pertinent political organ is also called for. In his actions, however, the director is entirely responsible to the working collective of his firm. In his external acts he is bound to uphold the general rules and laws regulating the participatory firm, such as those regarding taxation, financial reporting, and fulfillment of debt-service obligations.

Important changes have occurred in the legal, institutional, and policy setting of the Yugoslav economy since the early 1950's, but without exception they should be thought of as changes of policy instruments, rather than changes of the principles of participation. As such, they are of lesser importance for our present purpose, and we can omit them from our discussion.

Rather, let us briefly go over the basic defining characteristics of the Yugoslav economy in the light of the definitions of the participatory system presented in Chapter 2. Clearly, the first and most important characteristic, that of management by representative bodies elected by the entire working population of an enterprise on a one-man-one-vote basis, is fulfilled in Yugoslavia. And so is workers' participation in the income of the enterprise, together with the right of the working population to determine the way in which income is to be distributed, both between personal incomes and collective consumption, and among workers.

It is only as regards the position and generation of capital assets that, in terms of our third defining characteristic, the Yugoslav practice is slightly different from our theoretical model. Save in exceptional instances, the Yugoslav firm is not only a producer of its goods or services, but also generator of its capital. More specifically, the firms in Yugoslavia are called on to finance their investments—that is, plant and equipment—either from retained earnings or from borrowed funds, ultimately to be repaid from retained earnings. The assets of the firm thus can be divided into those derived from borrowed funds on the one hand, and those derived from reinvestment of income on the other. While comparable to "ownership" in a capitalist firm, the latter are not really owned by the collective, because they could not be withdrawn and converted into consumption (except under very special conditions).

This reliance on both self-financing and financing from borrowed funds differs from what we have given as our third defining characteristic of the participatory economy. On our definition all assets of the labor-managed firm are to be externally supplied, either by leasing of physical plant and equipment or, more realistically, by the borrowing of financial capital by the firm without the obligation of repayment from current income. The only obligation of the labor-managed firm in our case is the payment of current remuneration for the use of capital. While it can be demonstrated that the full external financing formula would be more desirable on several accounts, this should not be considered a major difference between the Yugoslav and our theoretical model. This is especially so because in one important respect all capital assets in Yugoslavia, whether derived from retained earnings or from borrowed funds, are treated as if they were all supplied externally. Namely, firms are required to pay a capital tax on all investments. Also, it can be shown that a considerable degree of self-financing in a participatory economy will constitute a definite hindrance to the efficiency of the entire system. Thus, to the extent that we find the actual performance of the Yugoslav economy efficient, we can conclude that it would be even more so with predominantly external financing.[1]

In the two remaining characteristics there is no major difference between the Yugoslav model and our theoretical one. The Yugoslav economy is unquestionably a market economy where all firms and households act to their best advantage, given the conditions in the markets they confront, and there is perfect freedom of employment in the sense of our definition.

When it comes to the motivating principle—which was compared to the motor of the system in Chapters 2 and 3— the confrontation with the Yugoslav reality becomes somewhat more complicated. We submit that by and large the principle of maximization of income per man is operative in Yugoslavia in the longer-range policies of the labor-managed firms, and especially if we think of the broader interpretation where income is not only monetary income. At the same time, it must be recognized that most Yugoslav managers and even most experts on the Yugoslav economy would deny the principle, or are unaware of it. Some will even be irritated at the thought of income maximization per laborer and consider it an unwarranted extension of the "inhumanities" of capitalism.

Without going into the details of the matter here, let it only be noted that the principle of income maximization per man, broadly defined, can be identified with several

[1] See my *General Theory of Labor-Managed Market Economies* (Ithaca, N.Y., 1970), in particular Chapter 14, section 9.

partial behavioral principles which are operative in Yugoslavia. Our contention is that if one does all the things that imply maximization of income per laborer, even unwittingly, one actually maximizes that income.

The first and probably most important such partial principle is that of what we may call efficient, or rational, utilization of raw materials, fuels, and other nonlabor inputs, including capital. This implies that the acting director, or executive board of the participatory firm, will use the inputs to the point where the last unit of the input costs him exactly what that unit adds to the value of sales. Obviously, if the earnings were more than the cost of the last unit, the employment of that input should be increased and thereby some extra net income for everyone in the firm would be secured. By contrast, if the earnings were less than the cost of the last unit of input employed, deletion of that unit would be bound to increase everybody's income. To allege that what we have defined here as efficient utilization of inputs actually is not practiced by the labor-managed firms in Yugoslavia is tantamount to saying that the labor managers and technical directors behave irrationally, preferring material losses over gains.

In this way, once the number of men participating is given, all inputs and thus the output of the firm can be determined, and income per participant will be maximized. The only remaining question is whether the size of the working collective is also governed by the principle of maximization of income per participant. Again, the answer for Yugoslavia is affirmative, provided that we think of longer-range decisions, and provided that we take the principle of maximization not as a mathematically exact objective, but rather as only approximate, as we have to anyway in any real situation. The common sense of this supposition is that firms in Yugoslavia which realize that they can considerably increase their incomes per participant by expanding their scale of operations (including employment) certainly will end up doing so.[2] Similarly, firms which realize that expansion would significantly impair their incomes per participant will refrain from expansion. But these two propositions—entirely sensible in my opinion —are all that is necessary to permit us to claim that the Yugoslav labor-managed firms actually maximize income per laborer.

This is equivalent to the demonstration of what we have termed in Chapter 2 the narrower interpretation of the income-per-laborer maxmizing principle. If we extend the concept to its broader interpretation, where the magnitude to be maximized need involve not only monetary income, but also incomes in kind or in the form of leisure and even the satisfaction from purely immaterial goods—perhaps even goods of an altruistic type such as giving employment to one's unemployed fellow men—then the maximizing principle, or the moving force of our theoretical model, comes very close indeed to the reality of Yugoslavia.

We can now turn to the main objective of this chapter, that is, the evaluation of the performance of the participatory system of Yugoslavia. The statistical indicators we are using are based on official sources, mostly statistical yearbooks of Yugoslavia.

As we have pointed out already, we want to familiarize

[2] The growth that we observe in Yugoslav firms is mostly of this type.

the reader with only a few of the most important indicators of performance of the Yugoslav economy, and compare them with the data for other countries. It is safe to
say that almost any economist who is interested in measuring the success of economic development would choose
some measure of the rate of growth of income or product
of the country. Because we are interested primarily in the
contribution of development to individual human welfare,
our basic index ought to be the growth of national income
per head of population. This, by and large, measures the
rate at which the real purchasing power of an average individual can expand, given the growth of his country.

For the period 1950–1964, we have data assembled by the
United Nations on the rate of growth of seventy-four
countries outside the Soviet bloc.[3] These, plus the fact that
world population grew at the rate of some 2.5 per cent, indicate that the world average of income growth per head
of population was for that period about 2.3 per cent. For
the same period growth of income per capita in Yugoslavia
attained the level of some 7 per cent. Because the first two
years of the period were years of complete stagnation—
caused by a blockade of Yugoslavia by its former allies
following that country's removing itself from the Soviet
bloc—it may be preferable not to include these two years
for Yugoslavia. This is also more adequate for reflecting the
performance of the labor-managed system, which was not
put into effect until at least 1952.

Thus, if the period 1952–1964 is considered, per capita
growth in Yugoslavia rises to 8 per cent, a rate surpassed
among all the countries of the world only by Japan, at 8.6

[3] See primarily the relevant volumes of the United Nations'
Yearbook of National Accounts.

per cent. If the lower figure of 7 per cent for the entire period 1950–1964 is taken, Yugoslavia is also surpassed by Israel at 7.5 per cent, and may be approached by one or two countries of Eastern Europe. But the latter supposition is based on official statistics which are usually questioned by western experts, and if western recomputations are used, the East European countries, including Soviet Russia, lag far behind the Yugoslav performance.

It may also be useful to note that the per capita growth of income in the United States over the fourteen-year period considered has been somewhere around 2 per cent, or about one-fourth that of Japan and Yugoslavia. We also should note that among the countries that we usually refer to as less developed, the figure of 8 per cent for Yugoslavia is second to none. A final observation on the question of per capita growth: if the longest conceivable period were taken for the participatory regime in Yugoslavia, 1952–1969, we would again come out with a lower figure of some 7 per cent. This decline from the 8 per cent figure for the period through 1964 is due to a two-year deceleration in Yugoslav growth after 1966, imputable to some major policy reforms which took place at that time.

It must be realized that high per capita rates of growth, however impressive they may be for Yugoslavia, are not a "pure" indicator of economic efficiency of a country. In fact, they are a reflection of two major attributes of the developmental effort: the efficiency of use of national resources, and the ability to generate savings, that is, to withhold national output from consumption and direct it into investments which, in turn, make possible further increases in output in the future.

The second of these two aspects of development effort

can be measured simply by the share of national production allocated to investment. It stands in Yugoslavia at some 28 per cent for the period 1950–1964, and is among the highest ratios realized in the world, both communist and noncommunist.[4] It is comparable to those realized in most command economies of Eastern Europe (including Russia); but it is remarkable because realized not in a command economy but in a decentralized market economy with a far higher degree of autonomy and freedom on the part of individual decision-makers. Among western market economies, it is again only Japan and Israel that attain the investment ratio of Yugoslavia.

Economists have several ways of measuring what we have termed above the *first* aspect of developmental effort—that is, how efficiently an economy uses its resources to produce national income and, by implication, economic growth and development. We will discuss here only the way which we consider most straightforward and most informative for our purposes.

The question can be asked, how much does an individual or a household get, in terms of growth of income, from every 10 per cent of income saved? The higher such growth, of course, the more efficient can be considered the performance of the economy in which the individual lives. For Yugoslavia we find that for the period 1952–1964, every 10 per cent withdrawn from consumption gave that household about 2.8 per cent growth of its income (and product). Of course, since the average household saved not ten but some 28 per cent, the aggregate rate of growth reached in Yugoslavia per household was 2.8 times 2.8 per

[4] This percentage excludes formation of stocks and inventories.

cent, that is, somewhere near the per capita rate of growth of 8 per cent noted above. The transformation from 10 per cent saving into a 2.8 per cent rate of growth over the period considered is again very favorable. It is about the same as for the two very successful economies of Israel and Japan noted earlier, and more than twice as high as that for the world combined, the less-developed countries combined, or the United States.

We can thus safely conclude that the economy of Yugoslavia under the participatory system has performed remarkably well, unsurpassed in a significant manner by any economy in the world, and about equal to the economy of the top two or three countries. If we add to these quantitative results the consideration that the Yugoslavs were developing by trial and error a unique economic system and were often forced to change considerably the economic policies designed to steer the economy because they had no coherent experience or planning model to go by, the picture becomes even more favorable. Moreover, it must be realized that the other economies that we used above for comparison, whether of the western free-market type or the Soviet command type, have been implemented for decades, in dozens of countries, and economists and policy-makers have devoted decades, if not centuries, to their study. It must also be realized that over the period of labor participation in Yugoslavia some degree of unemployment and labor migration to Western Europe have developed, the former largely owing to imperfect or incomplete long-range policies and planning. In the absence of these factors the growth performance of Yugoslavia would have been even more favorable.

Last but perhaps not least, we have casual observations of men living in Yugoslavia over time, and observations of travelers who are able either to compare the state of the economy with that of other developing countries, or to compare it at different time periods. These observations cannot give us exact quantitative measures, but they are almost invariably favorable. Nor should we neglect the fact that the economic, political, and social spheres are in fact interrelated. We will say much more about this in another context in the remaining chapters. To the extent that the influence runs from the economic to the other spheres, the influence of the participatory economy in Yugoslavia has indisputably been a good one.

5 ⤝⤝⤝⤝⤝⤝⤝⤝⤝⤝⤝⤝⤝⤝⤝⤝⤝⤝

The Participatory Economy in a Theory of Social Evolution

We are now in a position to approach the second major objective of our study of the participatory economy. As we have explained in Chapter 1, this objective is to attempt an integration of the phenomenon of a participatory economy into a broader context of history and social evolution. Besides its intrinsic interest, such an endeavor can help us in resolving or at least identifying a large number of concrete questions. Is the participatory system an accidental occurrence doomed to disappearance, or is it to stay with us and even to grow in importance? How is it related to other economic systems, not only in the context of economic performance but also in the broader sociopolitical conditions it engenders? And if the system is found viable and of enduring value, why did it not develop a hundred years earlier? These are only a few of the questions that we are led to ask as a result of the more confined economic study of the participatory economy.

In fitting the labor-managed economy into a historical and evolutionary setting, we may draw inspiration from what has become one of the main analytical approaches of economics: the *general equilibrium* approach. Two fundamental notions are embedded in the concept of "general equilibruim," both highly relevant for our purpose. First, there is the concept of equilibrium—and, of course, by contrast, disequilibrium—and, second, the notion that all the variables of a system are interdependent and exercise influence upon each other.

In economics, we say that a market system is in a state of general equilibrium if all variables, such as prices and quantities sold and purchased—while free to change—remain constant over time. But if one price is disturbed, this will affect buying not only in the corresponding market, but most likely in all other markets because people will tend to reallocate spending among all products. For example, a drop in the price of apples is likely to increase demand for apples and reduce that for oranges and increase that for apple-pie crust. Thus the disturbance in one market will tend to be translated into a general disequilibrium throughout the entire system because of the interdependence of spending decisions. And a new general equilibrium cannot be reached as long as even one market and one variable are not in a state of equilibrium.

Accordingly, any social situation—that is, a situation involving groups of men—can be seen as a state of social equilibrium or disequilibrium. The two may be distinguished by certain characteristics (analogous to those just noted in the economic context) to which we will turn presently. Moreover, such a state, in the sense of general equilibrium, is determined by the interaction of all the variables involved. There are no first- and second-order variables, the latter always determined by the former. With the exception of an ultimate origin and cause of all things (which we cannot treat of here and which everyone must seek for himself) all factors and forces, material, spiritual, moral, political, economic, and so forth, interact on a plane of equality, even if, at various times, with varying intensities.

As far as we can see into the past and the future, social history may be schematized as a transformation from one general equilibrium state into another. The transitional state is one of disequilibrium—or a number of successive disequilibria distinguishable in time and space [1]—caused by one or more specific disturbances to which we will turn presently. Of course the world of today belongs to the transitional state. This process of social transformation has a number of different dimensions—that is, it can be followed on a number of different planes, but for our purposes two are of greatest importance: the political and the economic.[2]

[1] An illustration may be useful. Toynbee's civilizations may be thought of as such distinguishable disequilibrium states. They can also be thought of as long-range cycles, whereas our theory, by no means contradicting his, attempts to provide the explanation for the long-range thrust of history. We will discuss this further in Chapter 9. See Arnold Toynbee, *A Study of History* (Oxford, 1957) or the abridgment in *Civilization on Trial* and *The World and the West* (New York, 1958).

[2] The moral and educational planes are also very important, and we will be bringing them into the discussion at many points, even if not in as systematic a manner as for the political and economic planes.

The fundamental postulate of our present analysis is that with respect to both of the two dimensions just mentioned, a *necessary* condition—note that we do not claim sufficiency—of an equilibrium social state is that of self-determination. In other words and more specifically, if a given society is to be in a state of equilibrium—that is, in a state capable of perpetuating itself—the members of that society cannot be divorced from the political and economic decision-making processes affecting them. On the contrary, they must be permitted to partake in these processes in the fullest possible measure. We are stating this proposition as an axiom; that is, we are not attempting to prove it. We can only say that it follows from the very nature of man, who is endowed with faculties of intelligence and will, and with a corresponding desire to exercise these faculties to the fullest. A little reflection—introspective or otherwise—should convince the reader of the plausibility of the proposition, or at least make him not reject it as a working hypothesis before familiarizing himself with the argument. In the rest of this chapter and the remaining chapters of our study, we will use this axiom as the foundation of our analysis. If we do not fully prove it, we will at least show it consistent with a large number of social, political, and economic phenomena, as well as with doctrinal trends.

Let us now put substance into the framework we have just created. We may begin by considering what we have termed above the "political dimension" of the social evolutionary transformation. We do so because (a) the treatment is comparatively more simple, and (b) because the economic dimension can better be discussed against the background of, and by analogy with, the political dimension.

The comparative simplicity of the political dimension resides—at least on the rather abstract and generalized level which we have chosen for this analysis—in the fact that what we have termed above the *necessary* condition of equilibrium can, *on the political plane* (that is, political self-determination), also be taken as the only condition. Of course, it is desirable to interpret "self-determination" as broadly as possible, implying, in addition to political democracy, a guarantee of human and civil rights and the absence of external limitation on national sovereignty. In fact, it is convenient to make a distinction between two aspects of—or more exactly, two distinct steps toward—the condition of political self-determination: (1) *macro-* or *outer* self-determination, corresponding to the absence of limitations on sovereignty—overt or concealed—from the outside, and (2) *micro-* or *inner* self-determination, corresponding primarily to political democracy and the guarantee of rights for the individual.

It is evident that the two types of political self-determination have seldom been reached by a given nation at the same time. The outstanding exception is perhaps the United States, where the revolution to secure outer political self-determination was predicated on the principle of inner self-determination. Elsewhere in the world, the development of modern nations has usually meant liberation from the outside interference of an elite, whether a ruling family or a political or military class. Only subsequently does democracy evolve into reality, after widely varying intervals and at widely varying speeds. The same is true whether we think of the emergence of the European nations in past centuries; or of Latin America, where the acquisition of

outer self-determination was by a national oligarchy; or of
the new nations of Africa and Asia, which have gained
their independence in this century, in many cases as pro-
claimed democracies but with a restricted political class.
Even in the United States, we are now aware that the
process from the enunciation of the principle of self-determination to its realization is far from complete.

It must be kept in mind that, in the spirit of the general
equilibrium analysis, the political and economic dimensions
are two aspects of one and the same phenomenon; this
implies, among other things, that a condition of equilibrium
fulfilled in one dimension is not sufficient for the entire
structure, that is, for an over-all equilibrium. Political self-
determination only indicates that specifically on the political plane there are no forces which would tend to produce changes in the general equilibrium. But of course
on other planes forces of change can still be present.

Let us now make a further step and consider the matter
in a historical context. To find the *initial equilibrium state*
on the political plane (as outlined at the outset of this
chapter), we must go quite far back in time—or, possibly,
in the direction of the most primitive human cultures of
today—into presocial human situations; that is, situations
where a man (with his more or less extended family) fully
decides on, or determines, all his affairs without being
constrained by the existence of other men.

As we have indicated already, the evolutionary process
was set in motion through a disturbance of the initial
equilibrium state. And one does not have to reflect for
long to identify this disturbance in the political sphere.
With an increasing demographic density, the frequency

of social contacts increased rapidly, and the necessity for political organization arose. Obviously, the rule of the fittest prevailed in the earliest and most primitive stages. Various forms of crude autocracy are thus historically the first modes of political organization that we encounter.

From then on we witness a long series of evolutions and revolutions on the political plane which took place because the necessary condition for equilibrium on that plane was not fulfilled (nor were some other necessary conditions, to be discussed presently, fulfilled elsewhere in the general equilibrium structure of society). It would be beyond our present purpose—and, indeed, beyond our limited capabilities—to present the whole story of this evolutionary transformation in any detail. However, we will use some instances of the revolutionary or evolutionary turning points later in our analysis—here and in the subsequent chapters—not so much to give a coherent picture of history as to substantiate the mechanics of our dynamic system.

The important point to be made here is that on the political plane, for some time now, more or less satisfactory forms of political self-determination are becoming perceptible in the world. Of older vintage are developments on the micro-level (of the "inner" type) in the form of political democracy and respect for civil liberties in countries enjoying outer self-determination. But we should not overlook the more recent developments on the macro-level (of the "outer" type) in the form of the gradual disappearance of colonialism and similar forms. Both developments are, however partial and imperfect, manifestations of the fulfillment of the necessary condition for equilibrium on the political plane. And indeed, there is no doubt that *on that plane* a state of equilibrium is gradually emerging in some countries, commensurate with the degree to which the condition is fulfilled. But of course it again could not be overemphasized that fulfillment in the political sphere is not the same thing as fulfillment in general, that is, in all dimensions of the state of society. Even a perfect political democracy—not that any such thing exists in the world today—could be subject to violent forces of change and actual convulsions stemming from nonfulfillment of necessary conditions for equilibrium in other spheres.

But let us now leave the political plane temporarily, and turn to the economic. For purposes of exposition we will first discuss the subject more or less in isolation, and only afterward attempt to integrate it into the broader general equilibrium setting. In fact, this integration is our principal task not only in this chapter but also in much of the remainder of this study.

What we have identified as the initial equilibrium in the political plane, that is, the presocial primitive culture, must also be our initial state on the economic plane. The necessary condition of self-determination is fulfilled in the primitive state not only in the political, but also in the economic sphere. That is to say, the individual supplies the wants of his more or less extended family, as a free producer, uncontrolled and unimpeded by anyone else. But can we say that the primitive state actually is one of the equilibrium in the economic sphere? Clearly, this would be so if the necessary condition of self-determination were also the only condition on the economic plane, as it was for the political dimension.

The conclusion is that the presocial state is one of equilibrium on the economic plane, although economic self-determination is not the sole condition. Because this statement involves something of great importance for all of our analysis, let us substantiate it quite carefully. It is at this point that economics is useful to us. Clearly, another general condition necessary for equilibrium in the economic sphere —especially in the very long run, which is our principal concern—is maximum economic efficiency; or at least, more realistically, the absence of gross inefficiency, given the resources and knowledge of a particular period. If at a certain point in time the economic system is significantly less efficient than it could be—given the productive resources, technological know-how, and state of economists' knowledge, and also given what other regimes, countries, or systems are achieving in the same period—that system is in disequilibrium, and natural forces of change will (sooner or later) set in and tend to correct the situation. The principal vehicles of these forces are market and nonmarket competition [3] and, most of all, the initiatives of socioeconomic reformers based partly on some kind of broadly defined "demonstration effect." Another powerful basis of disequilibrium and thus of change in the economic sphere is theoretical socioeconomic analysis. Marx and Keynes furnish perhaps the two most outstanding examples in this context, and we shall return to them later in this chapter.

We thus have two general conditions, both of which are necessary for equilibrium in the economic dimension. There is quite an interesting symmetry between these two conditions and the necessary and sufficient condition for equi-

[3] An instance of the latter is Khruschev's desire to catch up with the per capita national product of the United States.

librium in the political sphere: each of the two actually has two distinct aspects, as did the condition of political self-determination. In the case of the first necessary condition of the economic dimension, that is, economic self-determination, the analogy is complete. Here also, as before, we can speak of two aspects or steps, namely *outer* and *inner* self-determination. (The "macro-" and "micro-" denotations are perhaps less desirable here because they already have a different accepted economic significance.) As in the political sphere, outer economic self-determination implies that the activity of the enterprise is controlled and managed from within, and is free of external control, be it from the owners of capital, the government, or some other agency. By contrast, again as in the political sphere, inner economic self-determination implies participation in control and management by all who are active in the undertaking. It will be clear that the second step toward self-determination implies and is superior to the first.

We will return to the subject on more than one occasion, but even at this stage of our discussion it may be important —as well as interesting—to note that the distinction is by no means trivial or irrelevant for the real world. For example, the widely discussed phenomenon of the control of large corporations by management, about which Galbraith [4] and many others have written recently, is nothing but a case of outer self-determination with no inner self-determination. Possibly, the phenomenon is a major step in the process of evolution toward a full equilibrium in western economies.

[4] John Kenneth Galbraith, *The New Industrial State* (Boston, 1967).

The dual nature of the second necessary condition for equilibrium in the economic sphere resides in the duality of the concept of economic efficiency, and does not have the hierarchic or steplike character noted with the other conditions. The first, and probably the more important for our purposes is *allocational efficiency*, denoting how well a given economic system is capable of allocating its productive resources in producing national output.[5] The second type of efficiency we may most conveniently refer to as *distributional efficiency;* its various states of greater or lesser perfection reflect how well—in a normative sense—a given system performs in the distribution of national income among individual households. Clearly, both the distributional and allocational aspects of efficiency enter the second economic equilibrium condition, and must be satisfied for equilibrium. If in our subsequent discussion we put a greater emphasis on the allocational aspect of economic efficiency, it is (1) because of the normative, and thus nonobjective, nature of distributional efficiency, and (2) because imperfections of allocational efficiency generally are inherent in a particular economic system, and thus often cannot be eliminated without a basic change of system, as can—through taxation or otherwise—those of income distribution.

To return now to our exposition of the long-range evolutionary transformation, it will be noted that the presocial initial state also fulfills the second necessary equilibrium condition in the economic sphere. Indeed, when a man

[5] Economists will realize that the concepts of Pareto-optimality —both static and dynamic—and of the production possibility frontier are related to this first type of efficiency.

(with his family) is entirely on his own—when he is in the strict sense an individual and self-employed producer—it is only necessary to postulate rationality on his part to conclude that he will produce as efficiently as possible given, of course, his technological know-how and his resources). Of course, in the presocial state the question of distributional efficiency does not arise.

Self-determination and efficiency are the only two necessary conditions identifiable for equilibrium on the economic plane. And because they both obtain for our primitive situation, that situation is one of equilibrium on that plane. Moreover, recalling that equilibrium is also realized in the political sphere in the initial state, that state is one of *general* equilibrium.[6]

As was the case on the political plane, the initial equilibrium is also disturbed on the economic plane. To be more precise, on the economic plane the disturbance arises through the combined effect of disequilibrating forces already identified in the political sphere,[7] and new forces in the economic sphere. The latter, as the reader will easily understand, resemble the former in their "social" or "collective" nature and stem from technological change in the

[6] In fact it may appear paradoxical to speak of political self-determination in a presocial state where individuals or individual families do not experience any social contact with other groups. But the essence of the argument here is that in the initial state the individual experiences a full state of self-determination, in the sense that there are no other human beings who could limit his freedom of action in any respect.

[7] For example, such socioeconomic phenomena as slavery and the medieval feudal-military society resulted largely from the disturbance on the political plane.

direction of techniques calling for a more and more pronounced division of labor in a single productive unit. As in the political sphere the disturbance called for political organization, so in the economic sphere the necessity of division of labor in a single productive unit calls for economic organization among the participants within that unit.

Compared to the evolutionary transformation stemming from the political plane, the timing of the economic evolutionary cycle is delayed. Not only does the key disturbance of the initial equilibrium come considerably later in history (with the industrial revolution), but in certain productive sectors such as farming and the crafts, the initial economic equilibrium state has to some extent been preserved even in the most advanced societies. Also, as we will see throughout this study, the evolutionary transformation on the economic plane is considerably further away from its completion than that in the political sphere.

Turning now to the disturbance in the economic sphere in somewhat greater detail, we note evolutionary patterns analogous to those in the political sphere. Leaving aside the phenomena of slavery and feudalism, which, for our purposes, can be considered by-products of disequilibria in the political sphere, we find that the most primitive types of industrial organization assume the form of a capitalistic firm created and controlled by a single owner. This is a manifestation of the law of the fittest, often "fittest" primarily in the sense of "wealthiest" or "most unscrupulous," as in primitive times within the political sphere. With the forces of disturbance growing stronger and stronger, and development of larger and larger productive units—that is,

more and more pronounced division of labor—the corporate ownership-controlled form of production becomes
increasingly prevalent. In some parts of the world, con-
tinuation and further intensification of the same forces
gives birth to the giant corporation, where, primarily because of an atomization of ownership, we witness a transfer
of control to management.

A more detailed scrutiny of this process will be our
concern in the close-up view presented in Chapters 6 and
7. But even in this greatly abridged survey, one further
point may be made. In some parts of the world the disequilibrium forces in the economic sphere (i.e., lack of
economic self-determination and lack of efficiency, allocational as well as distributional) have become very pronounced at a time when the equilibrium condition in the
political dimension was not fulfilled either. The two forces
in collaboration then led to an abrupt revolutionary transformation. Unfortunately, this phenomenon of modern history, perhaps best epitomized by the Russian revolution of
1917, led—on our definition at least—to a new state of disequilibrium; in fact, disequilibrium in both dimensions of
our evolutionary general equilibrium structure. We thus
witness a pendulum-like movement from one disequilibrium
to another. Again, we must postpone the elaboration of
these theses (see Chapter 7).

Continuing with our analysis, let us consider the dynamics of the general equilibrium after the two major disturbances. Whatever the exact form of disequilibrium on
the economic plane, the social state in all its dimensions
must keep changing over time because of the disequilibrating forces on that plane. We have seen that economic self-

determination and efficiency are the necessary conditions of an equilibrium in the economic sphere. But a number of important questions remain: (1) do we know that there exists an equilibrium in the economic sphere consistent with the lasting forces which have disturbed the initial state? And if we do, (2) can we further be sure that the equilibrium in the economic sphere is consistent with that of the political sphere—that is, is a new (as distinguished from the initial) *general* equilibrium solution at all possible? Still further, (3) can we be sure that the solution on the economic plane will necessarily converge toward its equilibrium state? And if a positive answer to (3) can be ascertained, finally, (4) must the world progress or evolve toward an over-all general equilibrium or not? These are the questions that we must treat.

Using a somewhat more technical terminology, questions (1) and (2) concern the existence of equilibrium, while questions (3) and (4) concern the stability of equilibrium. As usual, the former—that is, questions of existence—are simpler to answer. In part this is because the earlier sections of the present study tell us a good deal about the existence problem and nothing or almost nothing about the problem of stability—stability being understood here, of course, in the broader context of our evolutionary theory and not in the narrower context of economics.

Let us direct our attention to the first question. It can be said that at least one equilibrium consistent with modern technology—or more exactly, one set of necessary conditions satisfied—does exist on the economic plane. In the first place, the labor-managed system as defined in Chapter 2 fulfills the necessary condition of self-determination. In fact, given the persistence of the forces which have disturbed the primitive initial state, I can think of no better way of realizing the first necessary condition.

While the first necessary condition of the economic dimension is identified with the definition of the labor-managed system, the second is found as what may be referred to as the most general derived theorem regarding that system. The theorem follows from the general economic theory presented in the companion study to this book, which we have attempted to summarize in Chapters 2 and 3.[8] It states that a labor-managed economy, given a minimum measure of perfectly feasible planning and economic policy, will perform at least as efficiently as, and most likely better than, any other economic system of today, even in terms of the strictest, purely economic, efficiency criteria. And once the criteria are broadened to include more humane, psychological, and sociological frames of reference, the labor-managed system comes out unambiguously superior. As we have seen in Chapter 4, these propositions certainly are not contradicted by the actual performance of the one national economy in the world today which approximates what we have defined as the labor-managed economy, that of Yugoslavia.[9]

[8] *The General Theory of Labor-Managed Market Economies* (Ithaca, N.Y., 1970).

[9] On the efficiency of the Yugoslav economy, see also my paper, "Yugoslav Economic Growth and Its Conditions," *American Economic Review*, LIII (May 1963). But given the uniqueness and the comparatively short duration of the experience of Yugoslavia, even if the results of the economy had been considerably less satisfactory, this would not have yielded a conclusive refutation of the above propositions.

The fact that the two necessary conditions for equilibrium on the economic plane are fulfilled simultaneously by the labor-managed economy deserves some further comment. It must be noted that this outcome is by no means an obvious one; I did not take it for granted at the outset of the present research. The outcome can be compared to a saddle-point solution well known in games theory. Observe that what we have called the economic dimension of the general equilibrium contains a number of possible states, each with a corresponding pair of attributes, one regarding the presence or absence of economic self-determination, the other regarding economic efficiency. The state identified as "the labor-managed economy" happens to realize the optimum—which is also the equilibrium condition—simultaneously for both attributes. If this were not so—that is, using our technical jargon, if the situation comparable to a saddle point were absent—an oscillatory and indeterminate solution, rather than a single equilibrium, might then be the only possible outcome. For example, disregarding for the moment the political dimension entirely, if capitalism were found to be most efficient economically, and labor management the equilibrium state from the point of view of self-determination (as is true by definition), a never-ending going back and forth between the two systems might turn out to be the outcome in the very long run, some countries adhering to one, others to the other in a given period.

We now turn to the second question posed above, which is the other question concerning existence. Specifically, is the equilibrium just identified in the economic sphere consistent with the equilibrium in the political sphere? In other words, can labor management coexist with political self-determination, and thus can the two "one-dimensional" equilibria form a full social general equilibrium? Clearly, if the two types of equilibria were perfectly independent, there being no conflict between them, the answers to both of these questions would be yes. The truth of the matter is that they are better than independent: in reality, they can be expected to be mutually reinforcing.

A whole treatise could be written on this positive correlation between economic and political self-determination. Here only a few main arguments will suffice. On the one hand, as regards the less-developed countries, producers' democracy will generally serve as an excellent schooling and inspiration for, and source of appreciation of the more remote and intricate process of political democracy. Also, and this may be even more important, it is an undeniable fact that the existence of social classes and wide income and wealth differentials in practice tend to give quite unequal real weights in the decision-making processes of political democracy. And if labor management does away with social classes and enhances distributional efficiency, these sources of imperfection should also be weakened or eliminated.

On the other side of the coin, once the advantages and general positive qualities of labor management are recognized, political democracy will provide an ideal vehicle, or environment, for that economic system. It is true that there is not an abundance of real cases on which these propositions may be tested; however, two instances should be quoted. There is absolutely no doubt that, compared to the Stalinist days of the late 1940's, the adoption of industrial democracy in Yugoslavia in the 1950's significantly enhanced political self-determination. A more recent, though more intricate, instance of the same type of interdependence is to be seen in the developments which led to the liberalization movement of early 1968 in Czechoslovakia. Moreover, at least in the case of Yugoslavia, the coincidence in time and interdependence between political outer self-determination and economic inner self-determination cannot be overlooked.

But even if there were no specific examples of the type given thus far, a strong intuitive argument still could be made in support of the thesis that a simultaneous realization of equilibrium conditions in both the political and economic spheres, and thus a social general equilibrium, is quite possible. Indeed, it should not be forgotten that what we have defined here as political and economic categories (primarily for purposes of explaining the mechanism of the system) still concern men, as integral decision-making units. And if, as is widely recognized, these men consider political self-determination—political democracy and civil and human rights—as an optimal state in the political sphere, it would seem to follow that they would not reject the same state in the economic sphere—especially if, as we have shown, the economic system is efficient. The reverse argument, not entirely tautological with that just made, can also be posited. If a certain group of men adopts and appreciates the advantage of economic self-determination, why should the same group reject political self-determination? Both arguments imply a coherence and unity of outlook, while their rejection indicates an absence of these qualities. We will use these arguments later in a wider context.

To sum up, we can answer the two questions we have posed concerning the existence of a social general equilibrium. Even given the forces which have disturbed the initial general equilibrium—that is, increasing demographic density and technological progress calling for more and more pronounced division of labor within an enterprise—a new state of social general equilibrium does exist. The specific instance identified is a combination of labor management in the economic sphere and self-determination (broadly defined) in the political sphere. We can now turn to the difficult and extremely important questions of stability—that is, to questions (3) and (4) stated above.

We recall that the first of these questions concerned stability within the economic sphere and the other the over-all stability of the general equilibrium solution. It is difficult, however, to isolate the forces operative in each of the two dimensions because, as we have noted already, there is a good deal of interaction between the two. Therefore, we will discuss the problem of stability only in the general context, but will bring in the distinction between the two dimensions wherever appropriate.

We have borrowed both the analytical concepts of a general equilibrium and the stability (or instability) of that equilibrium from modern economic analysis (which, in turn, adopted them from other, more exact scientific disciplines). At this juncture, however, we must recognize that this procedure is not entirely satisfactory for our purposes. The human—or social—phenomena that we are attempting to explain are far more complicated than those described by the scientific fields from which our concepts of equilibrium and stability were borrowed. Thus at least one additional set of analytical categories must be introduced if we want to discuss stability as applied to our present subject. We will distinguish between *inner* and *outer* stability.

Outer stability is akin to the traditional concept of stability as known in physics or economics, and simply describes a situation where an equilibrium, if disturbed, tends to re-establish itself. It thus resembles the case of a pendulum in physics, or a price in the vicinity of a stable market situation in economics. *Inner* stability can best be compared to a pendulum which is nailed down at its equilibrium position. In the context of a social situation this implies the existence of inner forces which are opposed to change— we may call them conservative forces—and which thus sustain a social equilibrium. They can do so with greater or less strength, just as the nail which holds the pendulum can be stronger or weaker.

While less conventional, inner stability can be shown without much difficulty to apply to our "new" social general equilibrium (we use here the term "new" to distinguish the equilibrium from the primitive state from which the evolutionary transformation originated). The very same forces inherent in basic human nature and attitudes that render the "new" social equilibrium an equilibrium are also the forces of inner stability. Introspection on the part of the reader can go a long way toward establishing this notion. The incurable pragmatist, however, may want to select a sample of individuals living in a political democracy and ask whether democracy should be relinquished, or ask the workers in a Yugoslav (labor-managed and income-sharing) firm whether they would

prefer to substitute for their way of doing things a capitalist or a Soviet form of business organization.[10] The answers
he will obtain will be so predominantly negative that he will
find it difficult to believe that such a consensus were ever
possible. So much for inner stability: once (and if) the new
general equilibrium is established, a very high degree of
inner stability is guaranteed; that is, it will be very difficult
to induce a society enjoying that equilibrium to forsake it.

We could not overemphasize at this point that what has
just been said pertains to a *general* equilibrium and not
equilibrium in only some of the pertinent conditions. In
the United States, more or less satisfactory fulfillment of
the necessary political condition is continually put in danger
of disequilibration stemming from the nonfulfillment of
other conditions, in particular those of distributional efficiency and economic self-determination. In the Weimar
Republic in Germany, as we will argue, such disequilibrating
forces from outside the political plane brought about the
disintegration of a democratic political order. Also, the
general equilibrium of which we speak here would have to
pertain to the entire world; otherwise, disequilibrium from
the outside of a state or nation would always be possible.

The question of outer stability is far more difficult, and
the answer—or answers—that can be given to it are less
clear cut. At the same time, the question is extremely important because it bears on, and indeed its answer contains,
the future evolution of social, political and economic conditions in the world. To provide such answers is obviously

[10] Actually, inquiries of this type were conducted in Yugoslavia,
and the results were unambiguous in the direction here suggested.

very difficult. Nonetheless, our approach permits us to carry the analysis somewhat further and to obtain at least partial results. We do so by way of a general outline in the present chapter, and provide more detailed elements of the analysis in the rest of the study.

The first thing that we must realize is that even the concept of outer stability (although we have suggested that it is closer to the conventional concepts of stability than is inner stability) is somewhat more intricate in its dynamic implications than stability in, say, economics. In the context of our present subject the difficulty is that the past and the future are not, as they are in physics and economics, perfectly symmetrical with respect to an equilibrium state. For example, a pendulum will proceed from a state of disequilibrium to its equilibrium position in one and the same manner, irrespective of whether it has previously assumed an equilibrium position or not. By contrast, a social general equilibrium involving people, people endowed with memory and ability to profit from experience, is a state the dynamic adjustment path to which will differ depending on whether that state has already been experienced or not.

Outer stability *with precedent* can in fact be considered only a variant of inner stability. This is true especially if the duration and extent of destabilization—figuratively speaking, the duration and extent of displacement of the pendulum from its equilibrium position—are unimportant. Without forcing the argument, we can thus extrapolate from the previous analysis, and assign to the (new) social general equilibrium the property of outer stability *with precedent* for minor displacements of "forced" shorter duration.[11] We emphasize here the qualification "forced" because, indeed, with inner stability there would not be any displacement unless it were forced from outside the system, subsystem, society, or group under consideration.

For displacements of wide amplitude lasting a long time (several generations), outer stability with precedent merges in its general properties into *outer stability without precedent*, because of the imperfect recollection and transmission of experience across generations. Therefore, it can be discussed with this last but by far most important category, to which we now turn.

On the most general level—that is, without any qualifications—hardly anything can be said; that is, we do not know whether the new social equilibrium possesses the property of outer stability without precedent, that is, whether conditions will tend to bring about the equilibrium or permit it to come about. If we make the specification *in the very long run*, then, for reasons which will become more apparent later, there is a strong presumption of this type of stability, *provided that* a cataclysmic short-run instability does not entirely destroy the social system; here we think of a major atomic conflagration or total moral decay, neither of which can be excluded as a possibility.

Even if the concept of stability used here is far more complex than the conventional concepts known in eco-

[11] For example, a country that already enjoys a full general equilibrium, including outer self-determination, might be subjected to a temporary disturbance originating from a neighboring dictatorship, its own democratic institutions being disrupted. If the external force disappears after a few years, the system will return to the equilibrium state previously experienced for a long period.

nomics, physics, or elsewhere, one basic element of analysis can be transposed into our discussion from the conventional sphere. Other things being equal, it can generally be expected that the forces of adjustment will be the stronger, the greater the degree of disequilibrium. Of course, we do not have here any exact quantitative measure of intensity, but rather a set of approximate indicators, based partly on how many of the necessary conditions for general equilibrium are not fulfilled, and partly on a qualitative assessment of the intensity of nonfulfillment of each.

The rationale behind this dynamic theory of social adjustment can be explained as follows. It can be postulated that people, as rational beings, either (1) actually see the three necessary conditions of equilibrium as reflecting an optimal state, or (2) if they do not have this understanding, for lack of information or experience, have nonetheless the capacity to recognize the necessary conditions as reflecting an optimum. And accordingly, in case (1), the farther away they find themselves from their ideal, the stronger the desire for it and the stronger the action they can be expected to take to attain it. In case (2), it can be argued that the greater the discrepancy between the *thus far unknown* optimum and the reality, the more likely it is that the optimum eventually will be recognized as such, and this will put into action the forces (present in case (1)) of adjustment toward equilibrium. A significant catalyst of the learning process in case (2) is what economists would call a demonstration effect. The American revolution and attainment of inner and outer self-determination in the political sphere two hundred years ago, the French revolution, and the economic self-determination of Yugoslavia today are some of the most prominent instances generating such demonstration effects.

The dynamic forces just identified are the principal "motors" of change and progress in the political and economic dimensions of our general equilibrium. But they are not alone in determining the path and especially the speed at which the systems move through history. Other forces, which we may call *conservative*, are present at all times, and are not entirely dissimilar from those which we have associated with *inner stability*. In relatively stable times they may be said to act primarily as friction- or viscosity-producing agents. On the other hand, in periods of rapid transformation or outright revolution, these (counter-revolutionary) forces can divert—or constrain—the transformation to a less than optimal path, that is, a path not leading directly toward the equilibrium situation. They can thus be the principal cause of a pendulum effect, already alluded to in an earlier example.[12]

One important source of these conservative forces is the strong desire of those who have brought about a revolution or a major transformation, and have thus become "the establishment," not to see the new state of affairs revert to what has been overcome. But this resistance to a movement in the backward direction unavoidably rigidifies the whole system in the forward direction as well. Among the many examples that could be quoted perhaps the clearest in this respect is that of Soviet Russia, where it took almost forty years after the revolution to overcome the con-

[12] As one example, see the analysis of the Russian revolution in Chapter 7, which brings out this point more clearly.

servative frictional forces before the system could move again—however slightly—in the direction of the general equilibrium solution. With a shorter time-period, the same will be observed in the other countries of the East European bloc. In Czechoslovakia, for example, the period of "frictional" stagnation (since 1948) lasted some fifteen years. But if the theory of equilibrium is correct, the conservative forces can only slow down, and never indefinitely stop or reverse the path of adjustment. With new generations coming in, and fading memories, the rational long-run forces—which are absolute, and not time-linked—must prevail in the end; when is only a matter of time.

Before continuing, a note on some of the international or geographic aspects of the subject at hand is necessary. If we speak of a general equilibrium, obviously, we must have in mind a full equilibrium in all parts of the world. Otherwise, with some of the equilibrium conditions not fulfilled in some parts, it would always be possible that through international "contamination," disturbances could also occur elsewhere in the world.

This postulate is less of a mechanistic transposition from some other equilibrium theory than might at first be suspected. In fact, it is only if all the necessary equilibrium conditions obtain in a given country or region—and especially the two conditions of self-determination (on the political and the economic planes)—that the danger of loss of outer self-determination for the other countries or regions disappears. Indeed, true and complete political self-determination on the national level implies the recognition of equal rights for others, including the right of self-determination itself, whether the others are at home or abroad.[13] By contrast, a dictatorship or an oligarchy in one part of the world, based on a disdain for the rights of fellow citizens, will generally have an even stronger inclination to oppression abroad than at home. In a similar manner, on the economic plane, self-determination—that is, self-management and income-sharing—which by definition precludes external control on the national level, will also be the best guarantee of economic control not transgressing national or regional borders.

Having explained the essence of our theory of social evolution, it may now be desirable to bring in the real world as we see it today, and attempt to interpret it in the light of that theory. We will do so here in very broad outline and reserve more detailed analysis for later chapters.

Realizing fully the hazards of broad generalizations, we will nonetheless attempt some. First of all we find it convenient to distinguish, for purposes of analysis, four categories of politico-economic systems in time and space. The first category contains only Yugoslavia since around 1950, as the sole representative of a labor-managed economy. The second we may call the western-type democracies, comprising most West European countries, the United States, Canada, Japan, and perhaps Israel for roughly the same period. The third category, represented primarily by Soviet Russia but also including China and

[13] The frequent meddling of the United States into the affairs of other countries on the political plane, in this context, is only an extension of an imperfect fulfillment of political self-determination on the national level. In many instances, such conduct is also the result of the absence of economic self-determination, with the "international corporation" calling for political shelter.

the East European "peoples' democracies," we can designate as socialist command systems. Finally, the fourth and most heterogenous group is that of the less-developed countries, whose principal common characteristic, besides their lesser economic development, is that they do not fit any of the other three categories.

It is now possible to construct a simple and approximate table, indicating for each of the four categories the degree of fulfillment of the three necessary conditions of social general equilibrium as we have presented and explained them in the earlier part of this chapter. Not to be too precise where precision is impossible, we overlook here the dichotomy of each of the three conditions, but we will refer to it occasionally later. We will denote the three conditions as P:I, E:I, and E:II, representing the equilibrium condition in the political sphere (political self-determination), the first necessary condition in the economic sphere (economic self-determination), and the second necessary condition in the economic sphere (economic efficiency), respectively. We will think in terms of three degrees of fulfillment. A minus sign ($-$) signifies nonfulfillment; plus-minus ($\pm$) mixed, or fulfillment with some serious limitations; and a plus ($+$) sign more or less complete fulfillment. Table 1 (p. 80) shows my tentative evaluation of *the period of the 1950's*. While system-category I is the principal concern of the present study, categories II, III, and IV receive a brief examination in the three subsequent chapters.

A few important qualifications regarding the table are immediately in order. First of all, we find for system I, Yugoslavia, a plus marking for economic efficiency, that is, for necessary condition E:I. While corroborated by the findings of Chapter 4, this should not be understood to mean that the economy of Yugoslavia is operating with perfect efficiency. Rather, the system has a potential for a high degree of efficiency. We also use the plus sign in this instance to reflect one of our key conclusions, the edge that the labor-managed economy has—in fact, in respect to both allocational and distributional efficiency—over the eco-

Table 1. Degree of fulfillment of necessary conditions for general equilibrium, 1950's

	Necessary conditions		
System-category	P:I (political self-determination)	E:I (economic self-determination)	E:II (economic efficiency)
I (labor-managed system)	±	+	+
II (western democracies)	±	−	±
III (socialist command systems)	−	−	±
IV (less-developed countries)	±	−	±

nomic systems of capitalist market economies, whose efficency we have marked as "mixed." The plus corresponding to the first necessary condition in the economic sphere (E:I) is a unique characteristic of the first system. We take the condition as being fulfilled even though there may be scope for significant improvement, because it can be said that self-management could not conceivably yet have had time to evolve fully over the comparatively short time it has existed. The plus-minus sign in the first column for the first system—that is, the limited fulfillment of the necessary equilibrium condition in the political sphere—may be more of a reality in respect to the 1950's, for which the table is constructed, than in respect to today.

Very little need be said about systems II and III (recalling that the table covers the 1950's). Primarily because of a comparatively satisfactory distributional efficiency, we feel that the "mixed" evaluation for condition E:II is most appropriate for the socialist command systems, category III.[14] Hardly anyone of good sense will dispute the nonfulfillment of the other two equilibrium conditions for system-category III, that is Soviet Russia, Communist China, and the East European socialist countries in the 1950's. With regard to system-category II, the "mixed" evaluation for E:II we have argued already, here and in fact in the earlier parts of the study, while the "mixed" evaluation for P:I appears fitting on account of serious imperfections in the process of political self-determination stemming from economic and distributional factors in most western democracies, on account of anomalies such as the "nonrepresentative" procedure of American political conventions, and most of all, limitations of rights in some countries belonging to the category, especially in the 1950's. Finally, the nonfulfillment of E:I in these countries is quite self-evident—in spite of certain partial or fragmentary tendencies in the direction of economic self-determination,

[14] It might also be argued that the command economy can be at least partially efficient in early stages of development. But it must be noted that Soviet Russia, the principal representative of this group, was no longer in that stage in the 1950's.

about which we will speak in more detail in the following chapter.

We come finally to the largest category, that of the less-developed countries. The determination of whether equilibrium conditions have been fulfilled here must be taken as highly tentative, not only because of the diversity of countries included but also because of the comparative difficulty in identifying exactly a particular set of conditions in a given developing country. The minus marking for E:I is the only one that is quite unambiguous (with the exception, perhaps, of a few cases—out of nearly one hundred). The "mixed" sign for E:II, that is, partial economic efficiency, again reflects more the "reasonable potential" than the actuality; and most of all, it is descriptive of the nonhomogeneity of the group. The mixed sign for P:I in category IV is nothing but an approximate "average" taken for all the countries belonging to the category. It should be noted that the partial self-determination that we here have in mind pertains to what we have termed earlier already the *micro-political* sphere; where self-determination means absence of colonial or other overt domination from outside (i.e., outer self-determination), obviously, the majority of the developing countries have today reached the equilibrium condition.

The analogy developed in this chapter between conventional general equilibrium analysis in economics and its sociohistorical transposition can usefully be pushed one step further. It will be noted that in the conventional analysis, as with a pendulum, there is generally an infinite number of disequilibrium points or situations for each equilibrium solution. Similarly, corresponding to the single point identified earlier as the *new* general equilibrium solution for society, we can think of a large number of forms that the disequilibria preceding the equilibrium state can assume. It is in the multiplicity of disequilibrium states, and in the transformations from one into another, that the interactions between forces emanating from the different dimensions can best be seen.

Some such important transformations—concrete evolutions, revolutions, and convulsions—will be studied in the subsequent chapters, in their respective contexts. There are others, however, which do not exactly fit our later discussion, but which are important and can be discussed at this stage of the argument as briefer illustrations of our multidimensional theory of social transformation. We will give three such illustrations.

The first that comes to mind is probably the most violent convulsion of the twentieth century, that of Hitler's Germany. Of course one cannot overlook the importance of the person of Hitler, but one can safely argue that without Hitler another like him could have come forth, while without the strong disequilibrium condition no one could have brought Germany and the world to the cataclysm that actually occurred. In summary manner, using our definitions and notations, the conditions that led to the Hitler convulsion can be characterized by the following six indicators:

$$\frac{P:I}{-\,+} \qquad \frac{E:I}{-\,-} \qquad \frac{E:II}{-\,-}$$

The first two pairs of signs reflect the state of the political and the first economic condition respectively, the first sign in each pair pertaining to outer and the second to inner self-determination, and the third pair reflects the allocational and distributional efficiency of the Weimar period before Hitler. Not being in a position—and in fact not needing—to make subtle distinctions, we use in this instance only the full plus and full minus evaluations.

Turning first to the minus sign for outer political self-determination, it can be seen to be the result of multiple forces. One was the occupation of the Rhineland region of Germany; another was the threat and fear of repressive Communist revolution (note that an international threat and resulting fear can be almost as much of an infraction on outer self-determination as occupation by foreign forces or as colonial rule); and still another was the reparations payments forced upon Germany after the First World War —whether paid or unpaid in the end.

The second sign, a plus, merely reflects that by and large the Weimar Republic did experience a state of internal political self-determination, including political democracy and respect of rights. In fact, it should not be forgotten that even the rise to power of Hitler was by and large constitutional. Although there were instances of outer economic self-determination, and even though workers' "codetermination" was a concept known in Germany of the 1920's, it is quite safe to use two minus signs with respect to the two components of E:I. Finally, the great depression with its enormous unemployment and waste of other resources can be interpreted as liberal (unmanaged) capitalism at its worst, and the two minus signs for allocational and distributional efficiency are therefore fitting.

The situation of pre-Hitler Germany was one of a very

serious disequilibrium, indeed. And the convulsion which
followed exceeded by far those conditions in intensity,
with, no doubt, the person of Hitler acting as a catalyst.
By the outbreak of the Second World War, Hitler had
transformed the characteristic indicators as follows:

$$\frac{P:I}{+\,-} \qquad \frac{E:I}{-\,-} \qquad \frac{E:II}{+\,+}$$

The last two plusses may be exaggerated but they certainly obtain if we want to adhere to a simple plus-and-
minus notation. We see here the interaction between the
various dimensions. Conditions unfulfilled in the preceding
state were transformed and fulfilled in the new state: Reasonable material well-being, jobs for almost everyone, and
restored national self respect, sovereignty, and strength
were exchanged—in a dramatic if not traumatic fashion—
for inner political self-determination. The economic self-
determination conditions, on the other hand, unfulfilled in
both stages, quite certainly acted as another catalyst, or
lubricant, in the convulsion. Indeed, had the German industries been under the democratic control of all working
in them—rather than just the few who hoped to gain a
great deal without losing much blood on the battlefields—
a far greater degree of stability would have been realized.
And perhaps, to begin with, Hitler might not have come to
power at all, because with labor management there might
have been no great depression in Germany and no support
or funds for his assumption of power.

But recalling that it is our task to illustrate our evolutionary theory, and not to rewrite history, let us not pursue
this line of argument. Instead, let us make an additional

point regarding the external situation. The outer self-determination of Germany, internally under a dictator, quite naturally led to the absence of outer, and in consequence, also inner political self-determination for many nations of the world.[15] As we have argued earlier, there is an internal logic in these developments, the disregard for and oppression of rights within the country being only naturally translated, in even stronger measure, into the same externally. The Second World War, then, was nothing but a new equilibrium adjustment stemming from this suppression of political self-determination of other nations, whether the suppression took the acute form of occupation in war, or only of fear and limitation of freedom of action imposed by self-defense.

Our second evolutionary episode occurred in the industrial western world at about the same time and as a response to stimuli—that is, disequilibrium conditions—not entirely different from those which engendered the Hitler convulsion. The state of allocational and distributional efficiency of western capitalism through the great depression was very much the same as that already identified for pre-Hitler Germany. In that period neither the distributional nor the allocational aspect of the second economic condition (E:II) was fulfilled. But this disequilibrium condition generated self-correcting forces which by the 1950's had reduced the degree of disequilibrium in both the allocational and distributional spheres. In symbols we can visualize this transformation as:

[15] These included among others Austria, Czechoslovakia, Poland, France, the Netherlands, Denmark, Norway, Yugoslavia, and to some extent Italy. Britain barely escaped at the cost of *blitzkrieg*, destruction, and heavy expense for armaments.

	P:I	E:I	E:II
Depression	$\pm \pm$	$- -$	$- -$
Transformation	$+ +$	$- -$	$\pm \pm$

The last pair reflects improvement in the two types of economic efficiency. This improvement can be associated with three major economic trends, or phenomena, in the decades which followed the great depression in the western industrialized world. The first two, primarily but not exclusively associated with the restoration of allocational efficiency, are the tendency toward increasing public power and intervention in economic matters, and the Keynesian countercyclical policy.[16] The third, primarily but again not exclusively associated with distributional efficiency, is what is commonly referred to as the welfare state, a development in public policy witnessed virtually without exception in western economies since the 1930's.

As we indicate by the change in the first sign in the two characteristic indicators above, there was also another force at work. Realizing that failure of outer political self-determination can also be a result of an explicit or implicit threat (or danger) from abroad, we must admit that in the 1920's and 1930's outer self-determination was far from perfect in many western countries on account of the increased possibility of a Marxist revolution. Indeed, in its cyclical and distributional patterns, western capitalism reached in the great depression precisely the state that Marx had foretold, and it was only natural that many people also expected the foretold consequences—especially with one large country, by then industrialized, already adhering to

[16] Primarily government deficit spending to prevent major declines in demand for goods, and thereby to prevent unemployment.

a revolutionary regime. The disequilibrium just identified for outer political self-determination then acted as an additional force to generate major economic reforms and corresponding adjustments in the economic sphere. As we have recorded, the partial resolution of the disequilibria in the economic sphere also contributed to an improvement in outer self-determination in the political dimension. Of course, the latter improvement pertains only to the episode which we have described above. It does not reflect the state of affairs in, say, the 1950's and 1960's, when other subtle imperfections can be discerned in the outer aspect of political self-determination. These make up our next and last illustration.

We are thinking, of course, of the general East-West tension which has developed since World War II and which has manifested itself most concretely in the "Cold War" and the many localized hot wars, revolutions, and other "minor convulsions." This state of world disequilibrium is in part a result of the individual disequilibria of the two main systems involved (our system-categories II and III). In part, too, it results from the incompatability—or differing nature—of the two systems, which in turn produces imperfections in outer political self-determination. These imperfections are in fact of two kinds: first, the threat to outer political self-determination, or "national security," felt by the focal countries—the United States, Russia, and China; second, within other countries by and large belonging to system-category IV, a real incursion on political self-determination as a result of an "outer-perimeter" defense strategy. In the latter context, the east European countries, Vietnam, Cuba, and the Dominican Republic come easily to mind, and the list could be lengthened with more subtle examples.

Of course, there is an asymmetry in the situation, the aggressiveness (or expansiveness) of the major powers being about inversely proportional to the degree of political inner self-determination, as recorded in Table 1 earlier in this chapter. The almost complete absence of economic self-determination in both camps, on the other hand, engenders or at least permits international economic expansion on both sides. And this in turn, whether by design or not, tends to reduce *both* the political and economic self-determination in third-world countries, thus further contributing to an over-all disequilibrium in the world today.

In fact, it is this difference of disequilibrium conditions in the major world systems that hinders or slows down most the operation of the fundamental long-range equilibrating forces which we have identified earlier. The long-run forces can be described as acting vertically in time, from conditions in a given system in one period to effects in the same system later. The intercategory forces of the type just sketched, on the other hand, can be thought of as *horizontal*, from one category to another, and thus frequently adding viscosity to the flow of history. The effect of the Vietnam war, a horizontal force, on the speed of long-range improvement in the social general equilibrium in the United States and in the world, and the effect of the invasion of Czechoslovakia [17] on the evolution of the communist countries of Europe toward a full equilibrium, are perhaps the most dramatic cases in point.

[17] Note that without the fear of the western world, the Russians might have been less precipitous in reacting to the Dubcek reforms.

6 ⟨⟨⟨⟨⟨⟨⟨⟨⟨⟨⟨⟨⟨⟨⟨⟨⟨

Western Capitalism and Political Democracy: A Close-up View

It is not our intention to deal with the subject of this chapter in great detail. What we want is to look at the historical phenomenon of western capitalism and political democracy from the point of view, and using the analytical method, outlined in the preceding chapter. We shall consider four broad questions. First, how and why did the initial disturbance in the economic sphere translate itself into a capitalist form of social disequilibrium? Second, how did western capitalism evolve through the two centuries of its existence under the influence and through the interaction of dynamic general equilibrium forces of the type suggested in the preceding chapter? Third, what actual and/or doctrinal role did economic self-determination, identified as one of the attributes of equilibrium, play during those two centuries? Fourth—and most important—in what specifically resides the imperfection, or disequilibrium, associated with the nonfulfillment of economic self-determination (i.e., of E:I) in the capitalist system?

The beginning of the period that we want to discuss—

that is, the moment when the disturbance in the economic sphere took place—is more conventionally referred to as the industrial revolution.[1] It is one of the most thoroughly discussed and analyzed periods of economic as well as general history, and we can hardly add anything to the general knowledge of the subject. What interests us is merely the question why, given the technical change which induced (for the sake of efficiency) formation of large productive units, involving cooperation of hundreds and thousands of workers, the capitalist form of organization emerged rather than any other one?

The answer is not difficult. From the social point of view, the class stratification which capitalism implied was at that time a perfectly natural and accepted state of affairs. And so was ownership of enormous assets by single individuals. Equally accepted, and inherited from the past, was the notion that ownership implies full rights of control. This notion was embedded in the teachings of Christian churches ever since Aquinas; possible limitations of the right of private property on grounds of social or public interests can be found in Church teachings only much later on.[2] Also natural was the procedure of hiring labor at a fixed wage to work on or with the property—whether land or capital—belonging to the employer. This was embodied in the legal codes of the period, all owners including capitalist owners being given the fullest and strictest protection of what were then considered their natural rights. In brief, all the institutional, legal, and attitudinal preconditions of cap-

[1] Cf. Chapter 5, p. 62.
[2] See Leo XIII, *The Church Speaks to the Modern World*, ed. Etienne Gilson (New York, 1954).

italism existed well before the technological and economic forces actually produced it. Thus, when the need for a large productive unit emerged as an economic reality, that unit could not have been other than capitalistic. In fact, as we will see, the capitalist mold into which the technological essence of the large firm was poured at the outset turned out to be so solid, in spite of its fundamental imperfections, that it took almost two hundred years before the transition to a further stage commenced at all. It would have been infinitely more surprising if in the days of industrial revolution there had emerged a firm based on industrial democracy, or any other type and form of organization other than capitalism. The point is so obvious that there is no need to elaborate on it further. We thus can proceed to the next subject, that is, the evolution of capitalism.

What has happened since the initial disturbance in the economic sphere in the countries it affected can be pictured in a nutshell as a set of causal interactions between the economic and the political spheres. At this stage it is convenient to distinguish—somewhat loosely—between what we may term *old* and *young* capitalist countries. The former include primarily the Anglo-Saxon and more advanced European countries; clearly, the distinction depends on when the industrial revolution occurred in a particular country or countries.

After the first stage of industrialization was completed in the old capitalist countries—that is, after the traditional (precapitalistic) nonfarm sector was absorbed and after the supply of labor ceased to be infinitely elastic at a subsistence wage—some of the fruits of increased productivity reached the working classes. The improved living standard, together with the experience of the industrial revolution itself, led to improved education and the potential of more intelligent and independent thought on the part of these classes. In a concrete manner, in turn, this engendered a quest for, and at least some achievement of, political self-determination.

On the plane of social thought a more or less well-defined resistance to, and condemnation of the nonfulfillment of the first and second equilibrium conditions in the economic sphere occurred in about the same period—that is, toward the end of the first hundred years since the industrial revolution in the old capitalist countries.[3]

As is well known, one branch of this train of thought, with Marx and Engels in the forefront, was more radical and combative, while the other, "utopian" branch, was milder, more conciliatory and, in a sense, more constructive; to the latter, containing among others the first germs of the participatory solution, we will return presently.

The more militant critics had indisputably a stronger impact on the later history of the then capitalist world. In the old capitalist countries, which are still our primary concern, the impact, while significant, was nonviolent and gradual. This can be explained by the fact, already noted, that by the time the social criticism occurred, the evolution toward political self-determination was well under way. Using the vehicle of political democracy it was possible to prevent the more extreme hardships that otherwise would have resulted for the working classes, and thus a safety valve, however imperfect, against explosive revolutionary situations opened up. Of course, it must be admitted that

[3] See below, p. 96.

the price that was paid in this way for prevention of violent change was the retention of less conspicuous evils, primarily those associated with the nonfulfillment of condition E.I. In the long run these evils may turn out to be quite damaging in their psychological and moral impact on the fabric of western societies.

In the old capitalist countries, which form the kernel of what today we refer to as western democracies, we thus find a spectrum of social phenomena all of which are the result of democratic self-defense by the working majority against a capitalist oligarchy in the economic sphere. The well-known concept of countervailing power, attained by the workers as an instrument against domination by capital or management; the various pieces of legislation to prevent extreme concentration of market power on the part of the wealthiest or most productive; the so-called "welfare state" are only a few significant instances that can be listed here as illustrations.

In the *young* capitalist countries, that is, in countries where the industrial revolution occurred considerably later —some hundred years later in Russia, the most significant member of the group [4]—the process just described with respect to the old countries could not take place, for lack of time, so to speak. Whereas in the second half of the nineteenth and early twentieth century, political self-determination was predominant and the precapitalist sector just about absorbed in the old countries, in the new countries the capitalist industrial sector was quite unimportant, political self-determination largely nonexistent, and the ma-

---

[4] Others were Germany and the central and eastern European countries.

jority of the population did not yet experience the basic disturbance of equilibrium in the economic sphere.

Even though these historical events occurred as much as one hundred years later in the new countries (actually more than that if China is included in the group), Marx, the year 1848, and the whole intellectual current engendered by the nonfulfillment of the two equilibrium conditions in the economic sphere were significant for both the old and the young capitalist countries simultaneously. The evils of capitalism in the second half of the nineteenth and early twentieth centuries may have been greater in the young capitalist countries than they were in the old. For one thing, note that for the young countries this period was still early in the industrial revolution, when in general there was no economic reason for the wage rate to rise significantly above the subsistence minimum, but those affected were only a small minority who had little if any chance of achieving basic reforms through democratic means. In other words, the safety valve which we have identified in the old capitalist countries did not exist in the new. Accordingly, the disequilibrium stemming from the nonfulfillment of economic self-determination and economic efficiency, with political self-determination also not fulfilled in most cases, had to lead to a series of revolutionary conflagrations—conflagrations whose outcome was by no means predetermined, precisely because those most hurt by the effects of disequilibrium were not in the majority. As is well known, a complete revolutionary turnover came about only in Russia, where, some may argue, the outcome was also conditioned by special conditions of war and the uncommon genius of the leaders of the revolution.

In Hungary, Germany, and elsewhere, similar revolutions were attempted without success.

But at this point we should leave the young capitalist countries, because Russia and later other members of the group ceased to be capitalist. It is from this juncture that we shall deal in the subsequent chapter with the Soviet-type command economies.

We can now turn to the third question proposed at the outset of the chapter, that of the position and role of economic self-determination in the capitalist world, from the industrial revolution to the present. For reasons which we will be able to explain better in a little while, it is convenient to organize our discussion into two distinct parts, considering first the more distant past and then the last two or three decades. Again, our aim is not to give a full historical account of the matter but to present a set of points relevant to our general evolutionary philosophy.

Perhaps a century after the industrial revolution, around the mid-nineteenth century, we encounter a significant critique of the emerging capitalist system. In some instances the criticism was formulated rather crudely, and in the immediate context of the evils of the period. This critique was basically directed toward the nonfulfillment of our two equilibrium conditions in the economic sphere. In particular, the inequality of income distribution and dehumanization of the labor contract were seen as serious drawbacks. Certain elements of the participatory economy as conceived in the present study can be found, among other places, in the writings of such authors as Proudhon and Marx. An event which had an important impact on Marx's thinking (and on many of his disciples later on) was the

Paris Commune of 1871, with its decree reorganizing industry into producers' cooperatives.[5]

On the side of actual implementation of the various reforms emerging from the critique, we find very few successful attempts during our historical period. This lack of success is often used as an argument to "prove" the nonviability of producers' cooperatives, labor-management, and other forms of productive organization designed to eliminate the state of disequilibrium on the economic plane. In reality, the lack of success was the result of many concurring forces—some of which we have already mentioned in speaking of the emergence of the capitalist system at the outset of the industrial revolution—which prove, if anything, that the sociopolitical conditions during this period were extremely unfavorable to the achievement of equilibrium. It is desirable to elaborate on this proposition.

First of all, there were all the legal, institutional, and attitudinal forms—the mold, as we have called it—inherited from the era preceding the industrial revolution which, once retained at the outset, were maintained, some even strengthened, by those with vested interests in the new regime. Second, there is the quite significant fact that any productive organization, capitalist or otherwise, needed then as now a certain minimum of highly qualified technical and organizational cadres. And for the vast majority of those eligible, then as now, it was certainly not well looked upon to join a "socialist" or other producers' cooperative. The social constraint was simply too strong for most to overcome, and the constraint may have reached powerfully—

[5] See Proudhon, *Qu'est-ce que la propriete?* (1840), and Marx, *The Civil War in France* (1871).

even if in a different guise—down into the workers' classes.

Another factor, not entirely dissimilar from that just noted, can be detected if we consider one of the positive aspects of early capitalism. Expansion of the new and highly productive sector following the industrial revolution clearly required a considerable degree of capital formation. But the latter could not be realized in a fully liberalistic situation without a very unequal distribution of income, favoring the capitalist and entrepreneurial classes. By contrast, any cooperative firm whose members, even if better off, still would have remained relatively poor, could never have hoped to realize the same savings from its total income as its capitalist counterpart. And because in the liberal nineteenth-century environment industrial growth depended heavily on self-financing, any isolated labor-managed or other cooperative firm would necessarily be at a decisive disadvantage with respect to a capitalist competitor.

A historical lesson can be drawn from the argument just made. Especially in the early stages of development, labor management must be supplemented by either a set of "rules of the game" forcing self-financing (as is the case in present-day Yugoslavia) or an extrafirm capital market nourished by other than autonomous savers' funds. We will elaborate on some of these matters in Chapter 8.[6]

If it is impossible to find a capitalist firm entirely financed by borrowed capital, it is because bankers or other lenders would find it too risky to fund the entire undertaking. And if the firm to be financed were labor-managed or coopera-

---

[6] This subject is also treated extensively in my *General Theory of Labor-Managed Market Economies* (Ithaca, N.Y., 1970), Chapter 14, section 9, and Chapter 15.

tive, the resistance to full or predominant outside financing would be even further compounded, for obvious reasons, in a basically capitalist environment.[7] This point suggests a whole spectrum of possible barriers or resistances that a potential or actual cooperative entrant had to face in the capitalist countries during our historical period. Since the cooperative or labor-managed firm was actually an embodiment of a negation of capitalism, in its business relations with the capitalist world—whether with buyers, suppliers, or creditors—such a firm necessarily and quite naturally had to be discriminated against. This factor is sometimes considered the most significant obstacle to producers' co-operatives in capitalist countries, even to this day.

A more subtle, but perhaps equally significant drawback of some of the early attempts for economic self-determination was that they remained, in some aspects of their basic organization, too closely influenced by the capitalist form. The fundamental philosophy of labor management was largely absent in these firms. There was not a basic comprehension that control derives from human participation in the activity of the enterprise and *not* from participation in ownership. Instead, members of the cooperative took part in the control and results of the undertaking by virtue of their participation in the ownership of assets, which necessarily led to innumerable difficulties, such as those resulting from entry or departure of individual members. This is not to mention the completely different spirit engendered by participation (in control and benefits) through owner-

[7] I elaborate on this matter in relation to what I call the "dilemma of the collateral" in *The General Theory of Labor-Managed Market Economies*, Chapter 15.

ship as compared with the participation inherent in labor management, that is, participation based on an activity in common.

Also it must be remembered that a clear legal form—comparable to a corporation, individual ownership, or otherwise—which would have reflected precisely the organizational aspects of a firm in which workers cooperated and shared in control and benefits, never developed in the historical period we are considering. And certainly we do not find in the same period very many lawyers and politicians who dedicated themselves to developing such a form.

But the two most important arguments explaining why economic self-determination did not take root to any significant degree remains to be made. First, it must be clear that a departure from the established capitalist form *en masse* and transition to a form based on economic self-determination would have been conceivable only under a major stress of material and moral hardship for the working classes. But as we have already argued—especially in the context of the old capitalist countries which form the vast majority of the world that we are concerned with—the sharpest edges of capitalism were lopped off through the democratic processes in the political sphere, and through some over-all material improvement.

The second argument is based on one of our important findings of Chapter 3. Unlike capitalist firms, the participatory firm will lose its impetus to grow before, or at the latest by the time it reaches, its maximum physical efficiency. This property of labor-managed firms, so salutary for competition and elimination of monopoly power, was bound to become a stumbling block when it came to the spreading of a labor-managed industrial sector starting from a limited number of firms. As the economic history of the nineteenth century shows so convincingly, capitalist firms and industries experienced no such difficulties. On the contrary, strong legislation was necessary in many countries to prevent the pronounced growth of individual firms from becoming cancerous.

This completes our tour d'horizon of the position of economic self-determination in the past; before discussing that of recent decades, a basic observation distinguishing the two periods is in order. In the past, the doctrines, attempts for establishment of economic self-determination, and corresponding failures almost without exception concerned a full-fledged application of the principles of co-operation, or self-determination. We can, therefore, speak here of a *total* approach. By contrast, at least in the capitalist countries, the recent period has been predominantly characterized by partial approaches to economic self-determination. By this we mean approaches which are far more modest in their aims and which are directed toward a transfer of a partial, often quite insignificant segment of control or influence within an enterprise to the workers or employees. The logic of this historical pattern is quite obvious. Having realized over the past two centuries how difficult it is to move from an autocratic or oligarchic to a democratic form of control and organization of an enterprise, those concerned are now exploring the possibility of gradual transition.

While these steps toward economic self-determination in western countries are only partial, they are widespread in their occurrence. Some of them are even institutionalized and embodied into law, and thus apply to entire countries. Works councils or works committees are required by law for larger undertakings (for example, the lower limit being fifty workers in France and as few as five in Germany) in a number of cases. These bodies have mostly consultative powers, but in some cases are entrusted with actual controlling or codetermining powers in special matters, such as welfare schemes or others; in the specific case of Germany these powers are quite significant, especially in matters regarding staffing and personnel.[8]

Recalling that the broad definition of economic self-determination must also include—as a necessary logical consequence—profit or income sharing, some might even want to argue that minimal self-determination is present in countries like the United States, where this practice has been introduced to a restricted degree in some corporations. The participation in profits can perhaps be taken as an indication of a general trend which eventually will bring about participation in decisions. The so-called Scanlon Plan is another form of participation by workers in management which has developed in the United States and has led to good results.[9]

While on the one end of the spectrum we have deliberate partial steps towards economic self-determination formalized into law, on the other side we can observe developments or occurrences which are perfectly spontaneous and

[8] See International Labour Organisation, Labour-Management Relations Series: No. 33, *Participation of Workers in Decisions Within Undertakings*, Documents of a Technical Meeting (Geneva, 20–29 November 1967) Geneva, International Labour Office, 1969.

[9] See for example William F. Whyte, *Money and Motivation* (New York, 1955).

often not even recognized for what they are. Of the many examples that could be given, two should suffice. The first is quite familiar to all of us in the academic profession. In many western institutions of higher education a large number of what normally are considered to be managerial decisions actually are made by the teaching staff, in a democratic manner. Indeed, those who have been participating in this democratic process of management are in an excellent position to appreciate the value of economic self-determination.

The other instance is less "pure"—in fact, it can be thought of as somewhat pathological—but it is far more significant than the first both in its extent and in the attention given to it in the professional literature as well as by the general public. For example, writing in 1966 in the *American Economic Review*, R. J. Larner finds (using, of course, definitions which might be questioned by some) that of the two hundred largest corporations in the United States, 85 per cent are actually management-controlled.[10] With the important difference that the number of people involved here hardly exceed one per cent of the members of the undertaking—as compared to the one hundred per cent required for full-fledged labor management—we have here a special (embryonic might be a better term) case of self-determination. We have already pointed to this phenomenon in the preceding chapter, linking it to Galbraith's work,[11] and offered it as an example of *outer* self-determi-

[10] R. J. Larner, "The 200 Largest Nonfinancial Corporations," *American Economic Review*, LVI (September 1966).

[11] John Kenneth Galbraith, *The New Industrial State* (Boston, 1967).

nation. The tendency toward management control is certainly gaining ground in the United States, and possibly in other western countries.

We have thus covered the first three questions raised at the outset of the chapter and are in a position to turn to the last and by far the most important one. This question concerns the nature of the disequilibrium associated with the nonfulfillment of economic self-determination in the capitalist system. The importance of the question should be self-evident; it was, indeed, a major reason for writing the present chapter. For a casual reader might say to himself, "Here is an abstract theoretical writer who pulls out an abstract theoretical general equilibrium model of social transformation and defines his equilibrium conditions; then when he comes to the capitalist system, finds one or more of his conditions not fulfilled, and thus starts calling my dear old perfect, eternal, and universally applicable capitalist system an imperfect disequilibrium state." It is to this reader, especially, that I owe a careful explanation of why I hold the capitalist state to be one of disequilibrium.

As suggested in the preceding chapter, the equilibrium which we encounter in western capitalist democracies can be identified as a quasi- or pseudo-equilibrium. That many people have the illusion of equilibrium is caused (1) by a fairly satisfactory fulfillment of two of the three necessary equilibrium conditions, political self-determination and economic efficiency (we have noted that more recently even distributional efficiency has been improved in many capitalist countries), and (2) by the fact that to a pragmatic mind, a recognition of imperfection generally is conditioned by a real experience of something more perfect, and this—save perhaps for the case of Yugoslavia more recently —is unavailable. But these observations on the formation of peoples' attitudes and opinions do not change the intrinsic quality—or lack of quality—of a given social state. Not even the existence of considerable affluence and wealth, experienced by many in the richest of the countries belonging to the group, can negate the fact of a basic social disequilibrium.

In the task that we have set ourselves in the rest of this chapter, we are helped considerably—by implication—by what we have done already. The reader will recall that the second half of Chapter 3 was devoted to a number of special dimensions of the labor-managed system which are not ordinarily encountered in other economic situations—the capitalist economy among them.[12] It is true that many of these qualities "feed into" our conclusion of superior economic efficiency (i.e., condition E:II) for the labor-managed economy—and by implication, comparative inefficiency of the capitalist arrangement[13]—but some of them really are nothing but an expression of the "human" or "humane" efficiency inherent in economic self-determination, that is, in the fulfillment of E:I.

We have also suggested earlier that the disequilibrium inherent in the nonfulfillment of the first condition on the economic plane is of a rather subtle nature. While this is true, and we will try to substantiate the notion in what

[12] The same subject is treated in much more detail in my *General Theory of Labor-Managed Market Economies*, Chapters 11–14.

[13] Recall that in our schematic representation we have expressed this fact by using plus and "mixed" signs for E:II and system-categories I and II respectively.

follows, it must also be recognized that the degree of sub-
tlety varies a good deal; actually the manifestations of disequilibrium at one end of the spectrum are quite straightforward. We will speak about the more obvious first, and
then proceed in the direction of more and more subtle and
less conspicuous ones, which in most cases are also the
more dangerous to society.

Perhaps the best known and most often quoted drawback
of capitalist production—which by implication results from
nonfulfillment of our first economic condition (E:I)—is
the inherent conflict which exists in modern firms between
labor on the one hand and ownership and/or management
on the other. The transition to an outer self-determination
does not change much in this context. In turn, this conflict
engenders inefficiencies, hardships, or other drawbacks of
many different kinds. The most obvious and conspicuous of
all are strikes and other acts of overt conflict between the
parties involved. Another difficulty, also well known even
if not always identified with the conflict within enterprises,
is the rigidity of money wage rates and other manifestations
of collective contracts which, while desirable from certain
points of view, may be quite undesirable from others. Indeed, without the rigidity of money wage rates induced by
the countervailing power of unions, there would be far less
unemployment in western capitalist countries, and far less
inflation. It is true that the state that would then prevail
might be even less desirable from the point of view of the
majority on the grounds of its distributional implications,
but we should keep in mind here that the standard of comparison to which we refer is not such an alternative situation under capitalism (a situation which, in fact, was wide-

spread in the nineteenth century), but an optimal equilibrium standard involving economic self-determination.

From here, we can go to some less conspicuous and only rarely recognized manifestations of the capitalist disequilibrium. One does not need to be trained in psychology to recognize a certain quality that we may call the "integrality" of the human person. This implies that in a normal human being his experiences, emotions, and general existence in one part of his life cannot be separated from, and will influence what happens in, the other parts of his life. If a man spends forty hours a week, and those the most alert and active hours of his life, in a work environment which is basically one of conflict (we recognize that normally there is no conflict with his fellow employees, but note that if there were, the case we would be discussing would be that of a hell, and not merely a social disequilibrium) then this conflict will spill over to influence the rest of his life and his general disposition. That man's life will thereby be less balanced and less happy.

Although I realize that someone may be able to produce examples to the contrary, my own experience tells me that this proposition is correct. If we do not realize it very clearly it is because in most cases the fulfillment of economic self-determination goes hand in hand with nonfulfillment of other conditions, such as, in most primitive societies, hunger, or lack of political freedom, which also contribute to human hardship. But if we find a precapitalist (primitive) society where economic self-determination is fulfilled without such alternative sources of human misery—Polynesian societies may offer a good example—we encounter a good deal more of human happiness. More tenuous, but in my opinion equally valid evidence is that of the pleasure and satisfaction of a traveler who after a month in New York City goes to spend a month in a traditional European village which, while not destitute, has not yet been tainted by capitalism.

While what has been said thus far can all be put under the heading of "conflict," our next subject can be discussed under the heading of "incomplete personality." Where previously "integrality" was our central concept, it is the notion of "fullness" that is of key importance here.

Indeed, the technological revolution which terminated the initial equilibrium in the economic sphere has deprived, through the resulting capitalist state, most men of their real creative and managerial (or organizational) functions, and only preserved, in most cases considerably dulled, his activity as a laborer.[14] We might say that what capitalism has done to the working man is the same as what the white man has done in America to the black man, what Marxist materialism attempts to do to the human soul, and what overuse of the automobile may do to the physique of the affluent American. All are forms of mutilation. This divorce of the majority of human beings from two out of their three roles of creator or co-creator then leads to unhappiness, alienation, and lack of fulfillment in general. In such countries as the United States, where productivity of and income from the remaining one function of the workingman has increased considerably, we detect a trend toward an apparently purposeless, self-centered, and materialistic civilization of affluence.

[14] We use here the term "real" to distinguish the functions from more or less artificial or "compensating" ones, usually referred to as "hobbies" or "extracurricular activities."

Ironically, in the western capitalist countries the average man is expected to decide through the democratic process about far-off peace or war concerning which he knows very little—yet he is deprived entirely of deciding on matters which concern him eight hours a day and about some aspects of which he knows more than anyone else in the world. In fact, the physical or mechanical degradation of work through the technological revloution must be compensated for by preserving the creative and organizational faculties of the worker. Codetermination and income sharing are both necessary conditions for reversing the unnatural primacy of material capital over human labor.

Looking metaphorically at the process whereby dollars of capital ownership control an undertaking, it is comparable in the political realm to a situation where the British (as absentee stockholders) would vote in American elections, Americans being entirely deprived of voting rights, and the British being allotted voting tickets according to how fat they are, rather than one per man. Using still another comparison, it can be suggested that if a capitalist enterprise is thought of as a single social body, then the conventional absentee control by the owners of capital make it into an externally manipulated robot. Evidently, under such conditions the oligarchic self-perpetuation of corporate managements referred to above is the only natural outcome. Whether such conditions are superior to the awkward rule of capital described by our metaphor is not always guaranteed; that neither arrangement is ideal, however, is evident.

The division between those operating a capitalist enterprise and those who control it, in another of its manifestations, brings us to a further set of observations. The fact that the capitalist enterprise is basically amoral, and that its activities may often be immoral, has a good deal to do with this division. We do not have to elaborate on this assertion of amorality and even immorality in any great detail. The aggressive promotion of cigarettes and smoking, years after the harmful effects of smoking were established; the findings about the share of responsibility that the automobile industry has in automobile accidents and fatalities; the exorbitant profits of some drug manufacturers, in many cases realized on sales to very poor men; and an advertising industry—used and thus approved of by the majority of other industries—which not only is quite willing to appeal to men's baser instincts, but which, and this is far more serious, has all but managed to erase the line between what is true and what is a lie, should be sufficient as sample evidence.

To say that all this results merely from the character of men who run these industries would not only be an oversimplification, but it also might be too harsh on these men. At least part of the explanation must be imputed to the system, that is, to the capitalist enterprise as an institution. The professional men who control a corporation, after all, have the responsibility to produce a maximum return (or value of stock, or rate of growth) for the owners. And if this objective can be attained only by amoral or immoral means, as long as these are consistent with existing law (or even sometimes if they are not), the majority of the managers will feel constrained to use these means. Such men will have not only the easy excuse, so often given, that if they did not behave as they do their enterprise would not withstand competition; but also, and more important, the

excuse that it is after all not they who are *responsible* for
the enterprise, but rather the owner or owners.

Now set this against a situation in a labor-managed firm
where, for example, a major advertising campaign based on
a more or less subtly obscene content is to be launched.
Whatever the moral standards of the one hundred per cent
who form the enterprise, they must realize that the corresponding responsibility and the public image that will be
created is entirely their own. And this, even if we postulate
identical intrinsic moral standards for the top one per cent
and the remaining 99 per cent in an enterprise, should in
many cases be enough to alter the decision about such a
campaign.

All this can have an extremely far-reaching impact on
the over-all morality of the capitalist countries—an impact
which in its ramifications goes well beyond the scope of
the present study. If a man ever since his childhood is exposed to advertising, a good deal of which is of dubious
quality and most of which has erased the line between true
and false, he may in the long run identify and confuse in
his own mind the values of "truth" and "lie" with the
values of "expedient" and "not expedient"—a confusion
which carried to the extreme is equivalent to the tower of
Babel. In its moderate, but quite real form, it then can make
more likely the occurrence of "credibility gaps" even in
countries traditionally dedicated to the defense of truth and
justice, and even with persons as highly placed as heads of
state.

Central in our concluding set of observations is the concept of the interaction of economic and political power. If
we agree that the ideal form of political self-determina-

tion—that is, perfect realization of our condition P:I—is one in which each individual is given equal say, then in the decision-making process it must also be agreed that interaction between the economic and political dimensions, with equilibrium not realized in the former, may bring about significant imperfections also in the political sphere. This can happen in two different ways. On the one hand, the working of capitalism in the economic sphere generally will permit and lead to a more unequal distribution of wealth and income than any other system. And because wealth and/or high income can generate excessive political power, the degree of equilibrium in the political sphere is bound to be diminished. On the other side of the spectrum, and often more dramatically, those who have no wealth and hardly any income most often end up having very little political weight.

The second link between the two dimensions, causing departure from the optimum in the political sphere, derives from the oligarchic rule developing in modern large corporations. That those positions at and near the top of management hierarchies in large firms carry a good deal of political weight—irrespective of the income-wealth attributes of such positions—hardly needs elaboration; the fate of thousands of workers and employees obviously depends on the decisions of those in the upper echelon. And if in a modern corporation there is virtually no check, whether by stockholders or workers, on those who hold the top positions, it follows that the democratic process of government will be distorted correspondingly by the fact that the desires and over-all outlooks of these men have a disproportionately high weight.

Thus it is both important wealth and important management positions in the capitalist systems that distort the democratic process of government from the ideal of equal weight for all. This distortion, more concretely, will deflect the course of a capitalistic country in the direction of the desires and outlooks of those who have economic power. If the qualities that brought the powerful to power were honesty, integrity, superior intelligence, and concern for others, one would not have to worry too much. But because the characteristics often required for attainment of economic power—whether in its "wealth" or in its "position" form—are materialism, individualism, disdain for spiritual values, and even lack of integrity and ruthlessness, the distortions that we speak about can be quite dangerous to society.

7 ‹‹‹‹‹‹‹‹‹‹‹‹‹‹‹‹‹‹‹‹‹‹

Soviet-Type Command
Systems: A Close-up View

As in the preceding chapter, the purpose of the present chapter is to examine a major economic system—or more exactly, a complex of related systems—in the light of the theory of social transformation laid out in Chapter 5.

The Soviet-type command economy is incomparably more complicated than the capitalist system; by the same token, it is also more interesting. As we have pointed out already, the state of disequilibrium involved here is much more complete and serious than in the capitalist system. But this means that the actual and potential forces of dynamic adjustment are also much stronger. Where before we were examining a fairly well-formed "geological formation," we are now facing an "active volcano" whose fumes are observable at all times, and which quite frequently erupts and can be expected to do so at any moment for some time yet. Moreover, there is today great diversity among the regimes belonging to the category which we want to study, and this differentiation is tending to increase.

The complexity of our subject is such that it does not

lend itself to categorization into separate "analytical boxes." Rather, we must deal with several significant threads which are intertwined and cannot be dealt with in isolation. It is thus important to organize the material and outline the ground which we propose to cover. Only in this way will it be possible, to a degree at least, to preserve the view of the whole while going into the details of the subject.

First of all, we must be aware of the time dimension of the subject. By definition, a state of disequilibrium implies a situation of flux, and thus to speak about a "Soviet-type command system" really is comparable to taking a snapshot of a moving object. We can permit ourselves to identify the system with one of its evolutionary stages as a first approximation only because that stage is very important and because it has lasted for a number of years. But a more careful analysis must be cast in terms of at least three distinct time periods. The first period, of course, includes the Russian revolution and its subsequent transitions, reaching approximately through and including the time of the New Economic Policy. The second period—the one by which we have identified this system—may be referred to as the Stalinist period. It reaches into the 1950's in Russia and the satellite countries. Finally we have the third or post-Stalin period, which again appears to be one of flux and transformation.

While recognizing the importance of the historical and evolutionary aspects of the subject, we find it expositionally desirable to postpone discussion of these aspects and stick for a while with the still picture of the Stalinist period. It is for this period that we must discuss, in more detail than in Chapter 5, the nonfulfillment or limitations of the three basic equilibrium conditions. As in the preceding chapter, we cannot make a claim of nonfulfillment of the necessary conditions of equilibrium without founding such an assertion on solid facts.

Only after we have established our "fixed point" by identifying the disequilibrium characteristics of the Stalinist era can we turn to the dynamics of the entire period, starting with the Russian revolution. This will involve first, in a separate segment of our analysis, the tracing of the transformations on the political and economic planes through the central Stalinist period, into the position already laid out in the still picture, and second, discussion of more recent evolutionary trends.

Through the stage of the present chapter outlined thus far, of course, our analysis is heavily—if not exclusively—focused on the Russian case. But beginning with the end of World War II, that is, with the later portion of the Stalinist period, an important part of the story of the command systems commences to be written outside Soviet Russia; and there is all evidence that in more than one respect the evolution of the satellites after World War II has played, and will increasingly play, a pilot role. In the same way as the Soviet-type systems branched off from the stem of capitalism early in the twentieth century, so did labor management and decentralization in Yugoslavia—the subject of the main part of this study—evolve as a new branch from the Soviet-type growth, through operation and interaction of the general equilibrium forces identified in Chapter 5. And even more recently, we have witnessed a series of transformations of different types, on different planes, and of different intensities in most of the satellite (or ex-satellite) countries.

All these can be integrated into the general setting of our theory of social transformation. An attempt at such an integration will occupy our attention at another stage in this chapter.

Our first task is comparatively the simplest. Indeed, the two minuses and one "mixed" indicator for P:I, E:I, and E:II respectively, suggested in Chapter 5,[1] for system-category III—identified here with the Stalinist period—are not difficult to justify. We will consider in turn each of the three necessary conditions of equilibrium.

On the political plane, Stalin's negation of self-determination, that is, elimination (or ridiculing) of political democracy and suppression of basic rights and liberties, was one of the most thorough in modern history. More will be said about the dynamics of this state of affairs elsewhere in this chapter; here let us recall only some of the salient static features. In elections, single candidates' lists and voting proportions in favor of such lists rarely descending below 99 per cent are self-explanatory, whether the results were obtained by compulsion of various kinds or by outright falsification. Secret political trials often leading to extreme penalties and political purges are other flagrant instances. Enormous concentration and forced-labor camps are another. Absolute limitation of foreign travel and almost complete limitation of internal movement, including change of job and so forth, are still others, as are the suppression of religious freedoms and the active persecution of all churches and religion.

Of course this extreme negation of political self-determination concerns what we have earlier defined as inner

[1] Cf. Chapter 5, p. 78.

self-determination. The condition of outer—or macro—self-determination was satisfied in the Stalinist period (by definition of a dictatorship). This however does not make matters any better, or make the over-all negative index assigned to P:I any less negative.

While the nonfulfillment of the first necessary condition of equilibrium on the economic plane in the Stalinist era is just as obvious as that of the political condition just noted, perhaps more can be said on its behalf that is not quite commonplace. In the transitional revolutionary period, as we will see later, the system passed through or "near" a stage which could be identified as satisfying our first equilibrium condition; however, by the time we come to the Stalinist period, the nonfulfillment of economic self-determination is *de facto* as total as it ever was. Actually, it can be said that as regards the economic self-determination of enterprises, the Stalinist regime retained all of the imperfections of the capitalist organization of production, and perhaps added others. An absentee capitalist control was replaced, but only by an absentee state control. We will speak later about the strictly economic implications of the phenomenon; it must be noted here, however, that from the point of view of control and decision-making this absence of outer and inner self-determination was considerably worse than that in the prerevolutionary capitalist enterprises because those holding economic power were now also vested with absolute political power. And thus, where before the revolution the capitalist was able to employ only economic sanctions against those forming the enterprise, the new state could use both economic and political—that is, penal—modes of constraint.

Everything considered, it can be said that in its Stalinist manifestations, the revolution led, from the point of view of the enterprise, to a condition which, in the suppression of inner and outer economic self-determination, was worse than conventional capitalism. It can also be said that in its philosophy, the system remained extremely capitalistic. The notion that control goes with ownership of capital was retained, and all that changed was the ownership—nominally from capitalists to the proletariat, but in fact from the capitalists to a bureaucratic state, or party, if we prefer, effectively run by a very few men. Those who went out to fight the scorpions in the revolution finally turned into snakes themselves. The humanely superior notion that control goes with participation—the concept underlying labor management, which was not absent in the early revolutionary days—was entirely suppressed and largely forgotten in the Stalinist days.

Because the Stalinist system can be assimilated to capitalism with respect to economic self-determination, many of the evil effects of a lack of self-determination discussed in the preceding chapter can also be discerned here, some in an even more pronounced form. In particular, what we have referred to earlier as the mutilation of men when used exclusively as mechanical factors of production, the deprivation of some of their integrally human faculties, is equally present in Stalinist state capitalism. Similarly, the evil effects of capitalism on human personality which we have associated with conflict within the firm, and which we have called lack of *integrality*, have their analogue in the system of the Stalinist era, accentuated by the complete absence of political self-determination.

Finally, we come to the third necessary condition of equilibrium, that of economic efficiency, and its at least partial lack of fulfillment in the Stalinist command system. This question of efficiency has been given a good deal of attention in economic literature. More specifically, *allocational* efficiency has been extensively examined. We will thus be able to survey the most important arguments advanced in this connection. Before doing so, however, a few words must also be said about distributional efficiency. The latter can be considered perhaps the brightest point—comparatively at least—of all the equilibrium characteristics of the system under study. Indeed, especially if we contemplate the period after World War II, both in Soviet Russia and other Soviet-type socialist countries, we notice an absence of distributional inequalities of the type that is encountered in many capitalist countries, even those enjoying considerably higher average incomes.

Equally satisfactory—and probably more important—is the distribution between present and future consumption and thus, in a sense, between present and future population, by means of current resources allocated to capital formation. According to some critics, the proportion of national product utilized in this manner is deemed excessive. On the other hand, Marxist writers, especially, see in the ability of the Stalinist regime to mobilize resources for development its greatest strength, or the dominant efficiency consideration in favor of the system.

Let us turn now to the question of allocation of productive resources within the Stalinist economy. Four major arguments can be put forth to demonstrate the comparative inefficiency of that allocation. The first, most abstract, and in a sense most theoretical, derives from the primitive version of the Marxist theory of value used in solving problems of resource allocation. The basic drawbacks of that allocational procedure—even if all problems of information, data availability, and computation are solved—are (1) that it involves average (rather than marginal) pricing and (2) that it does not take into consideration the existence of other scarce factors, in particular capital and natural resources. Especially in the context of a real situation where interindustry flows represent a significant proportion of gross unconsolidated national product, the inefficiencies resulting from the procedure, as measured by the difference between actual and maximum potential output of the economy, can be expected to be quite significant; and this expectation is further compounded by inefficient allocation of national product to final consumption, and in an open economy, by a nonoptimal trading solution.

The second argument is less theoretical, but equally as damaging as the first, if not more so. It is related to the command character of the system under study. Indeed, with an extreme reliance on central commands to individual economic sectors and firms, and minimal reliance on markets and decentralized producers' decisions, the computation alone of efficient central commands, while in theory conceivable, is in practice nothing short of impossible. And if on top of this we add the very serious and real problems of data availability and cost of data collection and data processing, the technical problem of administrative central planning transforms the whole Stalinist economy into a vast confusion.

While the first two types of allocational inefficiency are

more or less specific to the economy considered, the third is shared by the capitalist system. In its natural form the enterprise of the Stalinist period possesses very few, if any, incentive-generating qualities. Our comparison of the labor-managed with the capitalist firm in Chapter 3 [2] is fully pertinent here, the drawbacks of the Soviet-type firm being about the same as those of the capitalist firm in the context of incentives to labor, and in the context of incentives to management perhaps more serious. It is true that innumerable "artificial" schemes, ranging from the Stachanov program to various success indicators determining the returns to the director of the Soviet firms, were employed in an effort to overcome the natural absence of incentive; but many of them led to ridiculous distortions (e.g., very bad product quality if the indications were based on volume) and none of them was of an optimal nature.

The fourth inefficiency is shared by the command economy of Stalin's days with all other systems, but without any doubt it was of comparatively much greater intensity in the Stalinist system. It is the so-called interference of the state—or of *planners* or *policy-makers*—with the consumer's sovereignty to decide how to allocate the income and output which he has produced. With respect to the allocation between present and future the interference can be justified, as we have argued already. With respect to the allocation of expenditures between alternative types of present consumption, a justification is difficult to find; and thus we have another departure from the social optimum, imputable

[2] Cf. also Jaroslav Vanek, "Decentralization under Workers' Management: A Theoretical Appraisal," *The American Economic Review*, LIX (December 1969), 1006–1014.

to interference with the consumer's sovereignty. Considering that price rationing in the Stalinist era could involve price-cost distortions reaching into several hundred per cent, and that nonprice rationing was a frequent occurrence, we realize that the degree of departure from social optimum must have been quite significant.

The four types of inefficiency justify a negative index for the fulfillment of the *allocational* aspect of the second necessary equilibrium condition in the economic sphere.[3] Moreover, the first three have the specially unpleasant quality of becoming more and more pronounced as the command economy becomes more and more complex. Especially the second type of inefficiency, relating to the virtual impossibility of computing efficient command patterns, can be said to carry within itself the seeds of revision, if not of the destruction of the system at a more advanced stage.

This "prognostic of doom" calls for clarification. As long as a country can grow economically by doing more of the same, reproducing what has been done before—as Czechoslovakia did through the 1950's or Russia through at least a decade later—all is well, and often a rapid expansion is possible. But this method of growth, usually referred to as *extensive*, presupposes that the developmental sectors have access to unlimited sources of labor and/or land, with which to put into operation more of the same steel mills, truck factories, transportation facilities, or farms.

As soon as the "extensive" labor and land resources are exhausted, growth will be slowed down and stagnation must set in *unless* the economic system is capable of assimi-

---

[3] We recall that the over-all "mixed" index was used in the preceding chapter on account of *distributional* efficiency.

lating the newly arisen scarcities, and combining factors of production in fundamentally different proportions. Technological change, which no one had seriously to worry about before, now becomes the very life-blood of further development.

It is at this stage that decentralization (in its extreme and most effective form found in the participatory economy) acquires an absolute advantage, not merely a comparative one. It is a well-known fact that in the most modern and technically advanced firms an enormous proportion of time is devoted precisely to the development and adaptation of technology. It can occupy as much as 50 per cent of total production time. Now it is obvious that if all the planning, technical development, and adaptation were to be performed by the central planning authority or ministry, such central agencies would have to employ, in a country like Russia, tens of millions of people. And this is not taking into account the inefficiency of communication of instructions over long distances which this would entail.

The absolute absurdity of all this (the ministry would have to be about a thousand times bigger than the Pentagon!) and the implied necessity for real decentralization of economic decision-making are the most powerful guarantees that the "dark age" of absolute economic centralization must come to an end one day. And subsequently, we will argue later, an era of full political freedom and self-determination will gradually be ushered in.

But let us move now to the historical account and its chronology. Interpreted in terms of our analysis, the initial situation of the evolution we want to describe—that is, the situation in the years preceding the Russian revolution—is one of a pronounced social disequilibrium. Indeed, none of the three fundamental equilibrium conditions can be considered fulfilled. Although some first steps were being made in the direction of political self-determination, this was far from attained. On the economic plane matters were no better. Economic self-determination, that is, the first economic condition, obviously was not realized, nor was the second economic condition. A major portion of the economy actually was not yet absorbed into the modern sector and remained traditional, while a relatively unimportant industrial sector was subject to many allocational inefficiencies of primitive capitalism. Income distribution, on the other hand, was far from perfect throughout the economy. Moreover, it must be kept in mind that during the very last years preceding the revolution of 1917 the country was involved in a major war, and thus even the condition of outer political self-determination was violated.

The forces of transformation emanating from this state of extreme disequilibrium could hardly have failed to be violent. Eventually, they led to the two revolutions of 1917 and the whole period of transition between the initial conditions and what we have called the Stalinist period. The transition lends itself to an interesting analysis. It can be said to involve a pendulum effect as it leads from a state of total disequilibrium—that is, disequilibrium in all three necessary conditions—in the prerevolutionary period, which we may call A_{-2}, to another state of total disequilibrium in the Stalinist era, which is more or less the state identified for the 1950's in Chapter 5. The similarity to a pendulum is quite remarkable not only because we observe the passage from one to another extreme disequilibrium, but also, and perhaps more important, because there are clearly discernible signs of a rapid passage through an equilibrium point of the pendulum—at different times, in different forms, and with different durations for the three necessary equilibrium conditions. If we identify the period of transition as A_{-1}, and the Stalinist period as A, we have the following schematic representation for the three equilibrium conditions:

	P:I	E:I	E:II
A_{-2}	—	—	—
A_{-1}	±	±	±
A	—	—	—

where the plus-minus sign ($\pm$) is used to indicate the elements of equilibrium which can be discerned, often for a short time, at some point in the transitional period.

In accordance with our theory of dynamic convergence presented in Chapter 5, it can be postulated that at the roots of the social transformation which we call the Russian revolution was a vision of an ideal state which came quite close to what we identify as the equilibrium state. The temporary occurrences of what we have referred to as "elements of equilibrium" during the transitional period support this thesis. But it happened—and this may be the drawback of all revolutions—that once the dynamic forces emanating from that realization or "vision" were unleashed, it was impossible, for a variety of reasons, to control the phenomenon and lead it directly to an equilibrium state. We will discuss what we consider the most important reasons for this derouting in a little while. At present we have to pay some attention to the "elements of equilibrium" which occurred in the transitional period; some may not be known or not taken for what they are; hence they deserve attention.

Consider first the political sphere. The transitional positive elements of (inner) political self-determination—elements making us think of the passage of a pendulum through its equilibrium position—can be seen in two important phenomena of the Russian revolution. The first is that for quite some time preceding 1917 the revolutionary ferment was to a considerable degree nourished by aspirations for political self-determination. And what is more important, the first revolution of 1917, which took place in March of that year, and without which the Czarist regime could hardly have been dislodged, was the culmination and final expression of these aspirations more than of anything else. We thus have at the very heart of the transitional period the attainment of a regime, however short-lived, based on political self-determination.

The second phenomenon which should be noted is the so-called dictatorship of the proletariat by which the regime stemming from the second revolution of 1917 was to be governed. If there is any real correspondence to the somewhat unclear concept of "dictatorship of the proletariat," it is democratic decision-making by the proletariat, excluding other members of the society. But the group described as proletariat can be quite sizable—which renders the democracy within the proletarian class nearer a true political self-determination. More important, after the revolution of 1917 this restricted self-determination should in the long run have turned into a democracy of all once younger generations took over and the prerevolutionary class stratification disappeared. Indeed, it cannot be understood that government by the proletariat should forever mean government by those who were members of that social class at the time of the revolution.

Perhaps best known is the "equilibrium element" of the transitional period—recalling that it reached well into the 1920's—represented by the "New Economic Policy." This was a definite attempt to improve on the economic efficiency of the system. Unlike the equilibrium elements of the transitional period on the political plane, the NEP cannot be envisaged as a temporary passage of the pendulum through an ideal equilibrium state. Rather it is a desperate backward oscillation on the economic plane, occurring when it became clear that for reasons deriving from other dimensions of the social general equilibrium system, the ideal economically efficient state had been abandoned in favor of an inefficient one.

There were in the transitional period true equilibrium elements as concerns the first necessary economic condition, and by implication also as concerns the second. This is less well known, but certainly most interesting. One might perhaps go as far as to argue that if it were not for some of the special circumstances of the Russian revolution (to which we will turn presently) the system could in the 1920's have settled at or come near a participatory form.

We do not feel obliged to gather complete evidence in support of this contention. It is of interest, however, that Lenin, writing on the eve of the October Revolution of 1917, endorsed elected workers' bodies (councils) which would draw up the working regulations and supervise the management of enterprises.[4] The testimony of Professor

[4] V. I. Lenin, *The State and Revolution* (Peking, 1965), p. 131.

George Gurvich, who stood close to the revolutionary happenings and thinking, should also be noted:

In his first speeches, Lenin had announced that planning and a social revolution were possible only when founded on the fundamental direct representation of the workers. And I can even reveal a secret to you: the second program of the communist party, this second program which is absolutely impossible to find—you can look all over Russia for it, you can go through all the bookstores of France, unless you had bought it in May, 1917, you will not find it—this second program about which I don't know if all the copies were burned or eliminated, but what I can say is that it reproduced as principal points the same words of Lenin: no revolution and no collective planning is possible without the direct participation of the workers' councils and of their representatives. You can see that the idea of workers' self-management is there in its entirety. This did not prevent Trotsky and Stalin, who at that time were friends, from forcing Lenin's hand in the course of the war against the "white guards" and from leading him to suppress "temporarily"—I know the text very well—the workers' councils, under the pretext that they were preventing a sufficient production of arms. In the USSR, let it be noted, a paradox has remained: the peasantry, although always very reserved in its attitude toward the communist government, has benefited from economic democracy (kolkhozes, sovkhozes), whereas the proletariat, which is officially dominant, has not yet obtained what it began the social revolution with—workers self-management.[5]

[5] Excerpt translated from a lecture presented to a Brussels conference in honor of Proudhon, in part reproduced by Jean Dugignaud, "George Gurvich: Une Theorie Sociologique de l'Autogestion," *Autogestion*, Cahier No. 1 (December 1966), pp. 5–6. Gurvich's testimony is also confirmed in Branko Horvat, *Towards a Theory of a Planned Economy* (Belgrade, 1964), p. 101.

It thus appears that the derouting and slowdown of the Soviet progress toward full social equilibrium normally associated with the Stalinist period did in fact take its origin from Stalin himself, but as much as a decade earlier than is generally thought. We are also reminded by Gurvich that the then precapitalist agricultural sector did receive—at least in theory—the labor-managed status from the revolution. And in fact, a good proportion of the sector was able to preserve that status from then on.[6]

Gurvich's testimony is also useful for our next task. It suggests a historical basis for the pendulum-like movement, instead of a direct approach to equilibrium. The suppression of industrial democracy was deemed necessary in order to guarantee sufficient armaments for defense of the revolution against internal resistance and external intervention. Similarly, it was thought necessary to suppress political democracy and rights to eliminate the counterrevolution from participation in government. And finally, a system leading to efficient resource allocation could not have been permitted because that would have called for decentralization of economic decision-making, reliance on markets, and in general application of economic self-determination. In all three instances, the "ideal" objectives had to be given up

[6] In the context of our discussion it must be noted, however, that labor management was being applied here to a largely precapitalist form of production. Given the rudimentary state of technology, individual farming was very likely the most economically efficient form. The collectivization of farming in Russia thus hardly could be a success, especially in the early period where the disincentives from coercion and expropriation were stronger than the benefits, if any, from a division of labor. Of course, another reason for the comparative failure of collectivization was the complete absence of political self-determination and the resulting political interference with economic self-determination.

under pressure of external intervention. In addition to the external intervention *in space,* associated with limitations of outer political self-determination, we now discern also external intervention *in time* stemming from the prerevolutionary regime.

Moreover, it must be realized that we are facing here a situation which we have in our more abstract discussion identified as involving "stability without precedent." [7] We recall that such stability is of all types the most precarious, because the equilibrium state is something that no one in the system has experienced in actuality, and of which only some have had an abstract notion. Under these conditions, it can be argued, it was only natural for the system to overshoot the equilibrium and move again into a zone of disequilibrium. The hypothesis is even further strengthened if it is recalled that in its basic manifestations of lack of self-determination and inefficiency the disequilibrium of the Stalinist era had its precedent in the disequilibrium of the Czarist era. Thus for the majority the swing of the pendulum merely represented a return to, but nothing worse than, the hardships of the old days.

The tragedy of the transitional period, one may say, was the fact that the arguments against counterrevolution on which the suppression of an equilibrium state was based, which were quite real in the early years after the revolution, could still be used ten, twenty, and thirty years later, quite arbitrarily, by the few in power against any they wished to identify as the "counterrevolution." The story of the Stalinist era is basically the culmination of this process of distortion and falsification.

It is in this period that our analogy of a pendulum may

[7] Cf. Chapter 5, p. 73.

appear less satisfactory at first sight because the system had to wait some twenty-five years for a return movement, until the disappearance of Stalin himself. But it should not be forgotten that pendulums in fact move most slowly at the extremities of their trajectory. Moreover, and more pertinently, there is the influence of World War II, which is generally recognized to have had an internally stabilizing— that is, from our point of view, delaying—effect. And finally, there can be no doubt that Stalin personally had a considerable influence on the durability of the "Stalinist disequilibrium." Again with the exception of the war years, one can actually discern a certain over-all worsening of the disequilibrium, which suggests that the dynamic forces behind a social situation are a good deal more complex than those ruling the movement of a pendulum. One discernible departure from conventional dynamics is that the forces working to restore equilibrium tend to be cumulative over time. This produces a necessary intensification of the opposing forces used by those in power to preserve the disequilibrium *status quo*.

With the death of Stalin, of course, the temporary balance between forces of equilibrium and the official counteraction disappeared. In the subsequent fifteen years the equilibrium forces became predominant. Accordingly, our system-category III evolved, by and large, in the direction of equilibrium. The story now becomes a good deal more complicated, however, with an important portion of it now being written outside of Soviet Russia. We will turn to some of the specifics of this part of the story later on when speaking about the satellite countries. For the moment, let us disregard these complications and complete our evolutionary presentation of the command system of the Soviet Union.

As we have pointed out in Chapter 5, it seems that the leading force in the transformation process following Stalin's death was in the economic dimension, especially in the sphere of equilibrium condition E:II. Indeed, the economic inefficiency of the economy, unavoidably worsening with the complexity of an evolving command system, was the dominant reason for the post-Stalinist reforms. We also observe, however, some improvements in the sphere of political self-determination, including the civil and human rights. It is primarily economic self-determination that still remains the scarecrow of the regime.

The improvements appear to be, in a significant measure, a by-product of the attempts to enhance the efficiency of the economy. Thus, for example, one of the major prerequisites of economic efficiency is a greater measure of consumer sovereignty; but the latter in itself is simply one aspect of self-determination. More important, efficiency in practice calls for reliance on decentralized decision-making, markets, and the price mechanism. But all these imply a lesser degree of central administrative interference and thus, secondarily, an increased measure of political self-determination.

Eventually the Soviet authorities will have to realize that the truly optimal economic form calls not only for decentralization and markets, but also, on the level of the enterprise, for economic self-determination. And thus the quest for maximum efficiency, that is, for the fulfillment E:II, is bound to lead in time to the fulfillment also of the first economic condition. This applies irrespective of whether

economic self-determination is also recognized as philo-
sophically or morally superior to centralized economic control by the state. Only the timing can be affected—perhaps
significantly—by such recognition. The desire of the socialist economies to "catch up" with the western industrial
countries can only act as a catalyst in the processes just described.

A linkage similar to that outlined for the necessary conditions E:II and E:I can normally be expected—at least for
the Soviet-type regimes—between the first economic condition and the equilibrium condition on the political plane.
In the latter case, however, the relationship is somewhat
more complicated and thereby less predetermined; in fact,
especially in situations with a precedent of political self-
determination, a reverse order from P:I to E:I is not excluded.

The rationale behind this second linkage is quite simple.
A real appreciation of the rights of self-determination—
and a real taste for it—comes specially with the exercise
of that self-determination. Moreover, from an individual's
point of view, there is no fundamental qualitative difference
between the two types of self-determination. The two are
distinct only in that one type concerns what we might term
the professional environment, and the other the civil environment. And thus, if economic self-determination is experienced for a time and becomes a part of the society's
way of life, so to speak, it is only natural that in the course
of events a strong desire should develop for political self-
determination. If we speak here of a linkage in a specific
direction (i.e., from E:I to P:I), it is primarily because in
the Soviet-type economies E:I is likely to be realized sooner

on grounds of the first linkage; also, it must be noted that economic self-determination affects more deeply and more thoroughly a man's everyday life than political self-determination, even if the latter may be considered by him as important as the former.

To sum up, there is every reason to believe that the Soviet-type command regimes will transform themselves gradually in the direction of a full general equilibrium where all three equilibrium conditions, P:I, E:I, and E:II, are satisfied, and in greatest likelihood in the reverse order, from the last-mentioned to the first. In other words, we are arguing that for system-category III, the pendulum is returning, following the Stalinist swing, gradually but directly, to equilibrium position, without undergoing any further major swings. Of course, the timing of the process is virtually impossible to determine and nothing more definite can be said than that the horizon is one of perhaps as much as one hundred years.[8]

The prognosis for nonoscillation, on the other hand, appears a good deal more reliable. It can be argued—whether from historical inference or sociopsychological introspection—that systems are highly unlikely to return to specific disequilibrium states through which they have passed already; and the one major swing that could be envisaged for system-category III would have to be into something like the prerevolutionary conditions. The argument is germane to that which underlies the concept of stability with precedent, discussed in Chapter 5. Where a precedent makes it easier for a system to find an equilibrium condition, it makes it more difficult to return to a state of disequilibrium. More

[8] See also Chapter 9.

specifically, there is as little chance for the countries forming our system-category III to return to capitalism as there
is for them to return to a royal, czarist, or other extreme-
right political regime.

We are now ready to turn briefly to the more recent
story of the satellite countries. We include in that category
also the countries that were formerly dependent on Soviet
Russia, in particular Yugoslavia, but we leave out for the
moment China, which, it seems, represents a special case.

With the exception of Yugoslavia, it can safely be claimed
that none of the "revolutions" in the satellite countries leading to the Soviet-type regimes after the Second World War
was genuine in the sense that it was internally generated. Instead, as the term "satellite" indicates, the revolutions were
a result of a loss of outer political self-determination and
the imposition of its form of regime by a suzerain, because,
unlike the latter, they had lost both inner and outer self-
determination in the political dimension.

In the more advanced countries, the disequilibrium became much more serious also for another reason. The economic system which had to be borrowed from the Soviets
was far more inefficient in more advanced and developed
economies than it was in Soviet Russia, and thus the degree
of nonfulfillment of E:II was more serious. Moreover, the
degree of disequilibrium varied with the degree of political
self-determination which had existed prior to the forced
adoption of the Stalinist dictatorial regime, that is, with the
precedent of political democracy. The extreme case here is
represented by Czechoslovakia, where suppression of both
forms of political self-determination (inner and outer) could
be accomplished only at the cost of considerable terror, the

loss to prisons and to emigration of many able men, and for many years an utter degradation of the intellectual standards of the economic and political leadership of the country.

All these factors add up to a state of strong disequilibrium; the latter, in turn, explains the importance that developments in the satellite countries are coming to assume in the story of the Soviet-type economies. In some instances, it is no exaggeration to say even that they play a role of leadership. First and foremost we have in mind here the case of Yugoslavia, where, thanks to a much wider internal support of the revolution than in any other East European country—and perhaps also thanks to an uncommon courage—the process of reacquisition of outer political self-determination was accomplished only a few years after World War II, under the very angry eyes of, and in defiance of, the man in the Kremlin.

The Yugoslav case, which has assumed the dimensions of a third major world system, was even at its inception very interesting in several aspects. It foreshadowed in a rough outline patterns followed later by other East European countries. Thus, for example, the reacquisition of outer political self-determination—that is, of national sovereignty —was connected with reforms and fundamental changes also in other dimensions of the social general-equilibrium system. These accompanying reforms, in an environment of newly acquired freedom, aimed at a better adjustment of the system to the equilibrium conditions. In the Yugoslav case, the establishment of economic self-determination (that is, the fulfillment of E:I) was primordial. Also important was the abolition of that part of collectivization in agricul-

ture which was inefficient and an increased reliance on markets and the price mechanisms, both contributing to the
fulfillment of the condition of economic efficiency (E:II).
The significance of the first reform just mentioned is enormous: it at once represents the first realization of E:I by
any country in the world, and at the same time accom-
plishes a return—after more than three decades—to the
true spirit of the revolution of 1917.

Compared to the case of Yugoslavia, the process of reacquisition of outer political self-determination by other East
European countries has been much slower, and appears—
through the late 1960's at least—a good deal more anemic
and haphazard. Two distinctly different periods can be
identified here, coinciding approximately with the decades
of the 1950's and 1960's respectively. As for "anemia," the
phenomenon is quite understandable because those in power
tend to be in greater or lesser degree dependent for the
preservation of their position on external support by Soviet
Russia. To sever ties with the "metropolis" would, for
someone like Mr. Novotny in Czechoslovakia, have been
comparable to the viceroy of India severing relations with
"His Britannic Majesty" in the nineteenth century.

In the period of the 1950's we have witnessed a number
of attempts for national independence and other alterations
in the direction of equilibrium. But these without exception
failed in the sense that the alterations were not permitted
to go significantly beyond the degree of post-Stalinist liberalization also conceded in the "metropolis."

The events which took place in East Berlin, Poland,
Czechoslovakia, and especially in Hungary around the middle of the decade all share this character. Besides the fact

that Soviet Russia was then too near the days of Stalinist hegemony to permit dissent and diversification among other communist countries (i.e., countries ruled by a communist party), the comparative failure of these attempts can also be ascribed to the relatively high ingredient of purely nationalist and separatist motivation on the part of those revolting and, to a lesser extent, to a real economic crisis. Also, it can be said in retrospect that these occurrences were more spontaneous outbursts than well-prepared and thought-through reforms.

The events of the 1960's, insofar as they can be judged at the time of this writing, appear quite different. First of all, there was no full-scale repression of new trends and reforms in either the case of Rumania or that of Hungary. And in Czechoslovakia the spirit of the reform and some of its accomplishments could not entirely be extinguished even though that country had to undergo burdensome occupation by its "allies." Second, and this may be the cause of what has just been pointed out, the reforms stem from a very real economic crisis, and on those grounds can be defended as necessary by the leaders of the innovating regimes. Third, there seems to be more permissiveness on the part of Russian leaders with respect to "alternative" or "one's own" ways to socialism on the part of other communist countries. The last-mentioned phenomenon in turn seems to be an indication of further real as well as potential movement in the direction of equilibrium in Soviet Russia itself. A not entirely absurd hypothesis is that the Soviet regime is using—or giving additional freedom of action to—some of the more advanced socialist countries to explore the unknown waters which lie between itself and a loosely defined and largely unknown "optimal state."

Carrying the argument a step further, it can be said that the Soviet leadership, through its actions in Czechoslovakia, perhaps unwittingly got itself into a highly educational experience: if it insists today on the preservation of a non-market command regime which is entirely unsuited for an economy as advanced as that of Czechoslovakia, then it may be in for a dress rehearsal of the funeral of its own system ten or twenty years hence.

As we have noted already, the case of China is a good deal different from that of the satellite countries. First, there is its economic and demographic importance, which gives China a potential shared by none of the satellites. Second, the state of economic development of China at the time of the revolution of 1948 was considerably less advanced than that of the satellites. In fact, if we give sufficient breadth to our definition of the initial equilibrium in the economic sphere, we may say that prerevolutionary China actually experienced such a state (although this does not mean that there was a state of *over-all* or *general* equilibrium). At least on the political plane, the country experienced a "pendulum" movement similar to that experienced by Russia thirty years earlier; but the movement, perhaps because emulative, was a good deal faster, and no passage through an equilibrium point is discernible.

The important difference between the two focal regimes, Soviet Russia and China, is that there remains a significant time gap between the stages of evolutionary transformation. Retaining the image of a pendulum, it can be said that whereas the former country experiences by now a diminution of the space between the pendulum and its equilibrium

point, the latter country still is on the outward swing of the
trajectory. Since all great world powers—whether communist or not—have a tendency to consider themselves the
arbiter elegantiarum, and since generally they are too shortsighted to see things in their evolutionary context, we have
been experiencing the Russo-Chinese tensions and calumni-
ations of the 1960's. China fails to see in Russia a projection
of itself thirty years hence, and Russia fails to see in China
where it was thirty years ago; each terms the other a coun-
terrevolutionary traitor. The allegiances of the minor socialist states also, by and large, are governed by their state
or phase of evolution. Thus, for example, we find that the
only supporter of the Chinese way in Eastern Europe is the
country economically and otherwise least advanced, namely
Albania.

8 ≺≺≺≺≺≺≺≺≺≺≺≺≺≺≺≺≺

The Participatory Economy
as a Vehicle of
Economic Development

Following our examination of the two major world systems in the two preceding chapters, our present purpose is
to study what we identified in Chapter 5 as system-category
IV, the less-developed countries. The tenor of our discussion, however, will be quite different. Whereas in the preceding two chapters we attempted to identify the principal
characteristics of the two major systems and insert them—
so to speak—into our theory of social transformation, here
we will discuss the role which labor management could
play as a strategy in the transformation and development of
the countries of category IV. Indeed, in the former two
categories the countries involved are more or less committed to their present systems in the short run, and thus
our task was to take these systems for granted and interpret
them. In the case of the less-developed countries, by contrast, the present systems are widely varying and tend to be
rather undefined and fluid. What is given, and what brings

these countries together in a single category is their state of underdevelopment and poverty. In fact, using our nomenclature, many of the countries in question are experiencing, by and large, what we have earlier termed in Chapter 5 the primitive state, or primitive equilibrium, in the economic dimension. Our task is thus to study the role that labor management can play in the development of these countries.

If we assume a sufficiently long view—and assume no major cataclysms in the world—we can assert that society, including that of the now less-developed countries, will eventually attain the state of general equilibrium which, among other things, involves economic self-determination. But this is a rather esoteric proposition which probably no social scientist alive today will live to verify personally. Of much more immediate and practical interest is the question whether the participatory system can be the vehicle of development from the outset, or whether the less-developed countries must first pass through—and stay for a considerable time in—either or both of the two systems examined previously, before reaching the equilibrium state. The principal purpose of this chapter is to provide the background for the answer to this question.

We do not have to compare here the general merits of the three major systems in question; that has been done, explicitly or implicitly, in the preceding seven chapters of the study. Our present task is to examine the participatory solution in the light of specific problems of economic development: What are the advantages or disadvantages for a developing country in adopting such a system? The analysis must contain both absolute and comparative viewpoints.

More specifically, we must first show the intrinsic qualities
and applicability of labor management in the context of
economic development; second, the solutions must be compared with those offered by the other major systems.

We may begin our discussion by recalling certain fundamental notions about economic development in the modern
world. Probably the most basic one is that complete laissez-
faire will not bring to satisfactory development any of the
countries which have been considered as undeveloped or
less developed up to the middle of the twentieth century.
Some deliberate interference by the authorities in the economic life of these countries is a *conditio sine qua non* of
economic development. The task of the authorities, and at
the same time the general problem of development, can
conveniently be discussed under the following five major
headings. The order in which they are listed should not be
given any special significance, all five being more or less
equally important.

(1) *Accumulation.* It is necessary to accumulate capital
to increase average labor productivity, and thus income per
head of population.

(2) *Structure.* It is necessary to resolve several basic
problems of the optimal structure of the economy, such as
structure of output by principal sectors, structure of resource allocation, and so forth.

(3) *Foreign resources.* Every economy will need, in
order to carry out its development program, a certain minimum amount of foreign resources or foreign exchange
funds; the sources of such funds are exports, foreign borrowing, and foreign aid.

(4) *Training and education.* Most of the populations of
the currently less-developed countries do not possess the

education and skills necessary to the attainment of higher levels of development; attainment of such qualities must thus be built into the development process in an efficient manner.

(5) *Technical and administrative industrial leadership.* This requirement—identified with "entrepreneurship" in capitalist situations—is of such importance and distinct nature that it must be dealt with separately.

It is possible to think of each of the five categories as necessary conditions of economic development. Indeed, nonfulfillment or an unsatisfactory solution given to any one separately can act as a limiting factor or constraint on development, and thus nullify or seriously obstruct efforts to develop, however perfect and however thorough, undertaken in respect to the other necessary conditions. In consequence, the task of the authorities in leading a country to over-all economic development is not only to solve the scores of problems under each of the five headings, but also —and in fact, primarily—to orchestrate, as well as possible, the various tasks under all five headings simultaneously.

From the point of view of this study the five headings are useful in organizing our discussion. Under each heading, first, we may examine the solutions offered by or within the labor-managed system and also point out the differences, if any, between the three major systems. Second, on this basis, we can study the problem of "orchestration" of the five tasks into an integral development effort in a labor-managed developing economy.

(1) *Accumulation.* The labor-managed economy possesses a variety of means of accumulating capital, and, in respect to this task, is in a position at least as favorable as

any other economic system. Of course, in the primitive sector of a less-developed economy, which generally is quite
sizable, very little can be done except, perhaps, through indirect taxation at points where products enter or leave that
sector; export or import duties are the most significant possibility here. The modern, or development sector, on the
other hand, can well be tapped for further accumulation,
and there are certain instances where the labor-managed
system appears to have an advantage.

Among the means which we may designate as "forced,"
direct and indirect taxation of all kinds of the labor-managed firms can be used. Given the behavioral properties of
such firms studied in Chapter 3,[1] such taxation for the most
part will have positive incentive effects. Such effects will
largely be absent in other systems.

Also it must be realized that in a labor-managed economy
the enterprise is socially much more a part of the community where it is located than in any other system. Such a
relationship can be a strong factor in the willingness on the
part of the enterprise to accept locally imposed taxes (in
addition to nationwide taxes). Indeed, such taxes and social-
overhead capital derived from them will be considered, especially in a small community, as just another form of collective consumption. Actually, in the realistic context of
an underdeveloped country, the phenomenon just referred
to can be of primary importance for all social capital formation and over-all social advancement, because the labor-
managed enterprise most often will be the only modern

---

[1] A much more careful analysis of these matters is to be found
in *The General Theory of Labor-Managed Market Economies*,
Part III and Chapter 16.

and "surplus-income" generating institution of a village or other small community. In this context, clearly, a centrally planned system is far too clumsy an institution to handle the problems on the local level, while the capitalist mode of decentralization has, among its other drawbacks, a tendency to lead to the formation of different classes with ensuing divisions and conflict within the community. Also, in the capitalist alternative, there is no guarantee that most of the income generated by the enterprise will actually stay in the community.

Turning now to autonomous accumulation, it must be recognized that in a perfectly liberal capitalist atmosphere the savings potential of a less-developed country can be quite important, provided that, first, a capitalist-entrepreneurial class exists, and second, wide income and wealth distribution differentials are tolerable. This potential cannot, however, exceed the total income of the capital owners. By contrast, in a labor-managed market economy, where capital has the status of social ownership, the income share of capital can be autonomously withdrawn from consumption and used for accumulation (in the way explained in Chapter 3[2]), and in such a case the accumulation potential will be at least as significant as that postulated above for the liberal capitalist arrangement. Moreover—and this may be by far the most important consideration—in the participatory alternative, there is no analogue to the limiting condition just noted for the capitalist alternative.

In addition, as has been the case in Yugoslavia, individual firms can be called on to finance themselves fully in the

[2] See also *The General Theory of Labor-Managed Market Economies*, Chapters 15, and 18.

long run, by requiring them to repay outstanding loans out of income. An alternative, and perhaps even more attractive, possibility for a less-developed country is a tax (income or other) with the option that it need not be paid if the corresponding funds are utilized for expansion of capacity in the field of the enterprise or another field. Besides fostering accumulation, this procedure guarantees the spread of technical and managerial know-how *pari passu* with accumulation. More will be said about this subject under heading (5). We will also have occasion to speak about accumulation in connection with foreign resources under heading (3).

(2) *Structure.* Perhaps the most important fact with respect to the problem of a correct structure, noted already in its general context in Chapter 3, is that the participatory economy is in effect a market economy. Consequently, both the planners and the individual economic decision-making units have an objective basis for action. Moreover, the individual and decentralized actions of all decision-makers taken together, if rational in the sense that maximum income for everyone is sought, will bring about—or in a realistic dynamic world, will tend to bring about—maximum output and maximum social satisfaction within the economy. In other words, the labor-managed system will tend of itself to produce an optimal structure of the economy.

More specifically, thinking of realistic situations where a less-developed country is starting, so to speak, from zero, the market will provide each potential entrant into a developmental sector with a set of data which will guarantee him that his action, even if taken without any consultation with the central authorities, must be at least approximately correct. And in a typical development situation where contacts of provincial towns and villages with central authorities are difficult or almost nonexistent, decentralization based on markets may even be a *conditio sine qua non* of a regionally balanced development. It is in this particular context that the participatory economy has an important advantage over a centrally planned command economy, and is equally as efficient as a capitalist market economy. Of course, the latter will generally suffer from other comparative drawbacks—some already noted—which will tend to disqualify it as a means of development in the provinces. More about this will be said under heading (5).

It must also be noted that the capital market of a labor-managed economy will normally possess qualities which will make it particularly easy for the planners and policy-makers to design and develop an efficient structure of the economy. Indeed, having the control of a substantial portion of the capital market—for both short and long-term funds—the authorities will normally be able to influence the allocation of investment funds in the desired directions. In this context the participatory alternative approaches the maneuverability of a command nonmarket economy, while possessing efficiency properties largely absent from the latter.

Of course, the prices on which the optimal structure of the economy is to be based must be market prices consistent, as far as possible, with external or world markets. While the problems raised by an optimal price structure are quite general and common to all economic systems and thus need not be discussed here, one significant aspect of the problem belongs to our present discussion. It is often argued, not incorrectly, that through one policy or another a developing country should temporarily establish prices more favorable to certain developmental industries, in order to make them viable without price distortion in the long run. The great strength of the labor-managed system in respect to this so-called infant-industry argument is that part or even all of the cost of the infant-industry stimulation can be borne by the working population (membership) of the particular industries. Indeed, given the substantial share of labor in the income of most industries, the laborer-managers can make a decision to work temporarily with lower incomes provided that in the long run their incomes will increase. Again, it takes only a little reflection to realize that a comparable flexibility of solution does not exist in a capitalist situation, and that if imposed in a command economy, it may be strongly resented by the workers and act as a disincentive.

The last problem which we wish to classify under the heading of "structure" is one of the most critical problems of western-style economic development: the problem of large-scale unemployment and lack of job opportunities, experienced by so many less-developed countries. It is here that the labor-managed alternative possesses one of its strongest comparative advantages.[3] In a nutshell, the argument is that in a liberal (western-style) situation the au-

---

[3] I should like to express my thanks to my colleagues, Solon Barraclough and Tom Davis of Cornell University, whose discussion and analysis of unemployment in Latin America led me to these conclusions.

thorities who desire to induce entry and industrial expansion have recourse—or acquiesce—to measures which at the same time unavoidably lead to abnormally high use of capital per unit of labor. Hence, with a comparatively small and slowly growing stock of capital, there is a low level of labor employment. By contrast, the labor-managed developing economy, which also requires deliberate stimulation of entry and expansion of industrial capacity, normally can attain its objective without any distorting side-effects on the ratio of capital to labor.

To be more specific, consider for example the preferential foreign exchange treatment given to imports of machinery and other capital equipment so often used in developing market economies to stimulate entry and industrial expansion. This in turn reduces the project costs and—if factor proportions are at all variable—the labor-capital ratio and labor-employment. Perfectly analogous is the effect of high inflation rates, in many countries (in particular in Latin America) in excess of the nominal rates of interest. Such a configuration of the two rates leads to abnormally low and often negative real rates of interest, and the latter again, while stimulating investment projects, are bound to lead to low proportions of labor to capital and unsatisfactory utilization of the national labor force. Some fiscal measures favoring the investor can also have similar effects. The important conclusion is that many of the economic forces stimulating entry and expansion in western-style developing countries at the same time produce very undesirable effects on employment.[4]

[4] The undesirable impact of such forces on the distribution of wealth ought also not to be overlooked.

In a labor-managed situation the stimulation of entry and expansion proceeds largely along different lines. We will come to this subject later in the context of the fifth "entrepreneurial" constraint. Here let it only be noted that the establishment and expansion of labor-managed firms are based on investment in human capital—that is, development of administrative and technical skills—reduction and shifting of financial risks, and in many instances on a direct social decision and instruction to newly formed working collectives to enter an industry. Moreover, and this point should not be overlooked, inflation with its undesirable effects identified above is far less likely to occur—or to be tolerated—in a labor-managed economy than in a western-type market economy. In the context of the employment-effects the comparative advantage of the labor-managed alternative can only be strengthened when and if the labor unions in a western-type situation keep wage rates at an abnormally high level, or the employers try to reduce risks or losses from strikes or other labor troubles by displacing workers through mechanization.

(3) *Foreign resources.* Considering the most important source of foreign funds, exports, it will be noted that in general the participatory economy is in a good position to secure such funds by virtue of the fact that, by definition, it must adhere to a price mechanism which—among other factors—must be consistent with world market prices. Also, on a more practical level, the decentralization of the economy will make it possible for individual firms, or rational and efficient groupings of such firms, to deal and compete directly in international markets. Again, in this respect the

situation is comparable to that of a less-developed capitalist economy, with a possible advantage for the participatory system residing in the greater flexibility of conditions that the labor-managed exporters can offer.[5] By contrast, it is a notorious fact that even more advanced command economies are plagued in their export efforts by noncompetitiveness, poor quality of product, irrational price structures, and bureaucracy.

Regarding the other two sources of foreign funds, foreign investment and foreign aid, the position of a developing labor-managed economy is more ambiguous and also more difficult to assess. The difficulty stems primarily from the fact that there are so many noneconomic, mostly political and psychological factors that bear on the situation. Looking at the problem first from the point of view of the giving or lending country, and considering public funds, the problem of a labor-managed less-developed country is that there is no major wealthy power or set of powers in the world which itself adheres to labor management, and thus there is very little scope for "wholehearted" external support of the type enjoyed by countries which are willing to subscribe to one or the other of the major world systems in existence. At the same time the situation should not be judged critical. For one thing, taking the stinginess of the wealthy countries in the late 1960's as a standard of measurement, any developing country can hardly receive less than it actually has been receiving, and that without

---

[5] Note for example that the range of prices within which the participatory firm can settle a contract is far wider than that of a capitalist exporting firm faced by a union- or otherwise-imposed wage structure.

adhering to labor management. But more positively, it can be hoped that the motivations of the advanced and powerful need not always remain primarily founded on shortsighted self-interest. Moreover, even with self-interest the principal moving force, there are reasons to believe that labor-managed developing countries would not be left entirely abandoned. There is the evidence, or experience, offered by the case of Yugoslavia, which has received substantial public funds from the West. Along these same lines it may be argued that a neutral, or "halfway" third world might well be more acceptable to the polarized great powers than a stratification of that world into friends and foes. This argument seems to be especially valid in the longer run, when it can be expected that a gradual convergence of world systems will become increasingly evident to men of state.

Still viewing the problem from the side of the lender, we can now consider private capital as a source of foreign exchange for a developing labor-managed country. Of course, there is the limitation that in the labor-managed country, capital ownership does not carry with itself control of enterprises; and this will certainly discourage some private foreign investors. However, this drawback for a developing country practicing labor management will be offset or even reversed by other factors. The first is that foreign investors (in particular firms who otherwise would engage in so-called direct investment) still can lend to developing countries on contractual terms, and can even send their own specialists or other workers to increase the security of their funds. Of course these men will participate in management and income with all others. Second, a foreign lender, like any other lender to a labor-managed firm, enjoys on the whole greater security for his funds and especially for his income. The latter is backed, so to speak, by the whole value-added of the enterprise, whereas normally, in a capitalist firm, in case of difficulties the wage claims of the workers come before those of the lenders. Finally, the security of a foreign lender is also enhanced by the fact that there is virtually no danger of nationalization or expropriation in a participatory economy because of its intrinsic system equilibrium. In a capitalist developing country such dangers are always present.

If the situation with respect to foreign loans and aid is mixed from the point of view of the lender, it is definitely favorable when compared with other instances from the point of view of the receiver or borrower. Perhaps the most important argument here is that the labor-managed economy need fear the interference of foreign capital with internal matters of the country far less than any other, the control of all enterprises, irrespective of financing, being in the hands of those who form them. And because there are hardly any other valid arguments against foreign investment from the point of view of the borrower besides that of interference with national sovereignty, the case of the labor-managed economy is strong indeed.[6]

Of course, in the final analysis, the economics of the

---

[6] Of course, this statement is made on the implicit assumption that the contractual returns on foreign investment are reasonable, comparable to the internal returns on investment in the developing country.

problem at hand should not be forgotten. Other things being equal, the returns on investment funds are likely to be comparatively higher in the labor-managed developing economy than in another market economy, and this ought to attract such funds from abroad. The argument is based on the relaxation of the assumption of identical labor qualities in different systems and the effects of incentives on the productivities of all factors, including capital.

The two remaining tasks of developmental design and policy both concern the human factor, and as such are of fundamental importance. By the same token, they are probably the most complex and least well understood by development economists and policy makers. We recall that the first of these tasks involves the problem of training and education—and in an even broader sense, may be seen to include the formation of attitudes toward development—while the other, no less important, is more narrow and specific and concerns entrepreneurship or its equivalent in the developing economy.

Before going into some of the detail of these two tasks, it must be made clear that the real strength of the participatory form of economic development lies in this "human" sphere; the possible advantages noted above under headings (1), (2), and (3) are trifles in comparison. The analysis on which the general conclusions here are based is quite extensive, and we will be able to go into it only superficially. However, a good deal of it is akin to what has been said in Chapter 3 where we spoke about the special dimensions and qualities of the labor-managed systems, irrespective of whether the country in question is developed or less developed.[7]

Speaking about the human factor in general, we may first call to mind the question of over-all attitudes in the majority of the developing countries. In spite of colonial rule, the traditions and the attitudinal environment encountered in many of the developing countries are quite unlike those that prevailed in England in the eighteenth century and later in other parts of the western world, and which made it so natural and easy for the capitalist form to develop there. Similarly, the general conditions in less-developed lands usually do not provide a good ground for a highly centralized command system of national economic management. In all such instances, which in the opinion of the present writer comprise the majority of cases, labor management appears to be the most natural and most easily implantable vehicle of economic development, in part also because it has not been tainted by the colonialist stigma.

But apart from such consideration, even if the conditions in the developing countries were comparable to those in the early stages of the industrial revolution in the West, it would still be highly commendable to aim from the very outset for labor management. With reference to capitalism, why start with an economic system which clearly leads to conflict, class struggle, and even in some cases hatred, if

[7] Also highly relevant in the context of the discussion which follows is *The General Theory of Labor-Managed Market Economies*, Chapter 14, section 4, where we examine the question of entry and formation of new firms in labor-managed less-developed countries.

there is a superior way of doing things economically, which, in addition, does not promote such social ills? On the other side of the spectrum, why should one recur to limitations of liberty and unnatural centralization of the Soviet variety in the early stages of development if one can do at least as well without them?

(4) *Training and education.* Turning now from general attitudinal considerations to questions of training and education, equally significant conclusions can be reached. In Chapter 3 we have already suggested and explained the importance that a labor-managed enterprise can play in educating its members, whether on the job or through an organized additional effort. In the real context of a developing country, where communities and villages are poor and public education inadequate or nonexistent, the participatory enterprise can become an extremely potent factor of training, advancement, and education. Especially for the older workers beyond school age, this may be the only natural way for individual progress and adjustment to changing socioeconomic conditions brought about by development. Compared to public education, this form of training has the additional advantage of matching automatically the needs for with the supply of specific skills.

Only a step further in the same direction brings us to an important argument which we have already offered elsewhere and which deserves restating. By definition, labor management means producers' democracy in very concrete matters of running the enterprise where one works. Thus the participatory enterprise can also become a very important "workshop" in democracy and can prepare its members for the exercise of true political self-determination, simultaneously or later on.

Of course, in very primitive conditions, even the more concrete and "narrow" exercise of labor management through producer democracy may be too demanding on the members of the enterprise, and in such circumstances temporary limitation of participation can be envisaged.[8] But the principle remains the same in such cases, the temporary measures being something entirely different from a fundamental nonexistence of economic self-determination in either capitalist or command-type undertakings. In addition, the principle of income sharing need—and should— never be restricted under any circumstances, however primitive, and thus that aspect of labor management will always have its positive impact on those forming the enterprise.

(5) *Technical and administrative industrial leadership.* It is a notorious fact that entrepreneurial, managerial, and organizational talents in the developing countries are, as a general rule, extremely scarce or entirely absent. Consequently, the planners of development must secure from elsewhere, or foster, such human resources. Moreover, they must be able to secure them at least approximately in accordance with the planned or prospective structure of the economy. Finally, they must be able to direct the entrepreneurial, managerial, and technical talent in the direction desired by the society.

[8] To give an example, in Chile powers of the workers' councils of the agricultural cooperatives (*asentamientos*) set up in the agrarian reform of the 1960's were shared with a representative of the CORA, the government agency on agrarian reform.

In this context the labor-managed economy is in a very good position. Once long-range development plans are drawn up, the requirements of highly skilled personnel can be projected, educational and training scholarships offered, and domestic educational facilities or foreign placements secured accordingly. As for the last step, the actual placing of the top personnel in the desired occupations, it can be done without great difficulty. On the one hand, the students and trainees may be told even at the beginning of their advanced education what approximately is expected from them once their studies are finished. And on the other, their conformity to the orientation of the development plan —provided that the latter is rational—will also naturally guarantee to them, through operation of market forces, an optimal income.

Many of the newly trained and educated top personnel of the industry will be called on—especially in the earliest stages of development—to organize new firms, or, using our previous terminology, to generate entry. It is at this point, as we have argued in Chapter 3, that the labor-managed developing economy possesses a great comparative strength. Not only is the process of securing high-echelon talent readily controllable from the beginning to the actual final placement, but it proceeds at all stages on the basis of mutual consent and never has to rely on coercion. Yet in the labor-managed economy, the process does not rely on extreme maldistribution of wealth as an incentive.

By contrast, in the capitalist alternative for development such wealth and income maldistributions are a *conditio sine qua non* of entry and thus of development. Moreover, the authorities (or planners) in the capitalist developing country will have far greater difficulty in bringing about utilization of entrepreneurial and managerial talent—even if such talent exists or even if it can be secured—in the desired directions. On the other side of the spectrum of alternatives, that is, regarding the Soviet-type command system, it must be recognized that the latter is in a superior position as compared to the capitalist formula in the purely mechanistic sense. Indeed, in a centrally planned economy, the control over and steering of the human factor into the education and then into the employment desired by the authorities should—at least in theory—be flawless. However, if a less mechanistic and more humane criterion is used, it becomes obvious that the system leaves something to be desired; and the experience of the existing command economies certainly only supports this contention. Moreover, the manager or director in the command economy goes out to the workers of his firm as an opponent, as does his capitalistic counterpart, in that he places other interests above those of the workers. Matters are entirely different in a participatory firm.

An over-all evaluation of labor management as a vehicle of economic development, based on its viability with respect to all five developmental tasks, thus comes out favorably both in absolute terms and in comparison with other alternatives. While in no respect is the labor-managed alternative significantly inferior to other ways of generating and promoting economic development, it is significantly superior in some aspects to either one or the other of the two major regimes.

With respect to the orchestration of the whole, that is,

how well the planners and policy-makers can harmonize all five tasks simultaneously in arriving at economic development, the labor-managed alternative also appears to be in a good position. In a sense it offers a maximum of efficiency, maneuverability, and flexibility, with a minimum of complexity. Whereas very soon after take-off the machinery of a centralized command system tends to become an inefficient and ever heavier ballast to the economy, the labor-managed alternative, efficient from the very beginning, tends to operate better and better as the economic system reaches higher levels of advancement and complexity. Where more or less liberal capitalism can fail entirely at take-off for lack of entrepreneurial and technical talent, or for lack of spontaneous accumulation, the labor-managed alternative has the capacity of solving similar difficulties efficiently, and of still tending, in the long run, to produce a developed economy superior to the capitalist.

Finally, it must be kept in mind that if an alternative way—that of capitalism or of the Soviet-type command economy (system-category II or III)—is adhered to at the outset of the development process, and later a changeover is made to labor management, considerable additional costs, tangible and intangible, political, economic, and social, will almost certainly be incurred. By the same token, all such costs can be avoided if labor management is adopted from the outset by a developing country.

9 ←←←←←←←←←←←←←←←←←

Projections and Convergence

Once the situation of the principal world systems has been evaluated for the recent past, the question logically arises: Where are they going? Can we form any expectations regarding the future development of the various systems, and their convergence, if any, toward what we might call a world general equilibrium solution? I realize the boldness of any attempt to predict such an evolution. Nonetheless, I feel that such a hazardous exercise can be useful. The outline that follows will necessarily be extremely sketchy and fraught with scientific lacunae. Still, there are some aspects of the important question of convergence that can be clarified. For the rest, it seems worth while for any concerned citizen of this precarious world to make an educated guess as his contribution to the discussion of mankind's future.

As our point of departure or initial condition, let us return to the state of the four system-categories in the 1950's as we have surveyed it.[1] We may further select a tentative

[1] See Table 1 (above, p. 80) and the surrounding discussion.

time horizon of some fifty to seventy years, through the first three or four decades of the 2000's, and, primarily in order to be able to think in terms of sequences of events, an intermediate period somewhere around the turn of the century. Starting from the base period, we can denote the three periods as A, B and C. It may well be that the timing of B and C as just indicated errs by a few decades or so; but this should not trouble us because what we seek here is a very rough picture, and especially an indication of chronology and intensity of change.

Recalling our simple theory of dynamic adjustment within the social general equilibrium, we first identify two comparatively steady systems, the labor-managed and the capitalist—our categories I and II. In the first of the two, the three necessary conditions for equilibrium are at least partially fulfilled, even in the 1950's. Category I, exemplified by Yugoslavia, experiences perhaps least a state of disequilibrium today, in the decade following the base period, because even the third condition, P:I, which we have identified as only partially fulfilled in the 1950's has come a long way toward fulfillment by the second half of the 1960's.[2] In fact, there is very little doubt that a full equilibrium, including fulfillment of P:I, will be reached in period B by system I.

Especially with the intense exposure to and experience with producers' democracy by the majority of the society, Yugoslavia should experience a rather smooth transition for

___

[2] Here we have in mind the far greater respect for human and civil rights, diminution of the exclusive powers of a single political party, and elections based on a choice among more than one candidate.

the rest of the itinerary that may separate it from the full equilibrium state. Of course, there always remains some danger of retrogression in the political sphere from external causes—that is, from the nonfulfillment of what we have earlier referred to as outer political self-determination; but this danger, for reasons that we will note later in discussing category III, at present appears unlikely.

In fact, as I see it, the problem in Yugoslavia today is the practical working out of a mode of full political self-determination, in a new situation, where the fulfillment of the equilibrium condition E:I becomes a part of the way of life, a part of a fundamental law, which is not called into question by political groups, factions, or parties as a matter of the day-to-day democratic process.

The perspective for equilibrium in category II, and in particular for its most significant representative, the United States, appears in one important respect less promising. The problem seems to be that in category II, but again especially in the United States, we are witnessing a state of what we might term *quasi-equilibrium*, resulting from a complacent satisfaction over the partial fulfillment of P:I and E:II, and a negligence of E:I.[3] The reasons for this state of affairs are quite clear. On the positive side, a pragmatic civilization such as that of the United States will not be convinced by theoretical argumentation of the type presented here or elsewhere; if anything can generate a movement toward equilibrium in E:I and improvement in the other conditions, it must be a strong demonstration effect— and that for the moment is missing and will be for some time. The example up to the present time of system-cate-

[3] See Chapter 6.

gory I—an experience full of experimentation and even of some setbacks—is not enough. Moreover, the label of "socialism" will be a sufficient taboo for many years to come to prevent or slow down change.

The negative experiences, such as the problem of the American poor, the Negro question, the distress and purposelessness of American young people, on the other hand, cannot easily—and certainly will not willingly—be traced to the nonfulfillment of E:I. The reluctant action in the sphere of P:I is at best a partial solution; and the only partially accepted medication of the "welfare state," through its emphasis on distributional efficiency, is aimed at condition E:II, but entirely leaves out the more fundamental, but at the same time more subtle condition E:I. For the working man, who is now not much more than a "factor of production," fulfillment of E:I implies the restitution of his status as a full-dimensional human being, participating with all his faculties in the determination of his socioeconomic fortunes.

The progress from a mixed fulfillment of P:I and E:II in period A to a complete fulfillment in the subsequent periods is likely to be considerably faster and also smoother. This belief is based on the observation that there are existing channels and institutions—primarily the democratic process itself—which can serve, and in fact have been serving in the decade following period A, to advance the degree of equilibrium of the two conditions in accordance with the dynamic forces of adjustment outlined earlier. And there is no reason why the trends should not be continued into the future periods B and C.

Nonetheless, as we have argued above, the over-all state

of category II carries within itself a strong dose of inertia.
This is not to say that the full general equilibrium will
never be reached by countries of category II, but simply
that it will be only very late, most likely not before period
C, and very strong friction, especially with respect to E:I,
against its achievement can be expected in particular in the
United States. In other countries belonging to category II
(e.g., France and Germany), the process may be much
faster, the speed of adjustment being proportional in part
to the ability for self-inspired socioeconomic reforms, in
part to the intensity of exposure to other systems. To state
the expectation in perhaps an extreme version, it can be
said that all or most of the world outside of the United
States may have to have attained equilibrium condition E:I,
and even to have reaped its fruits for some time before the
United States will move, by virtue of a diminished weight
of its capitalist traditions and of a demonstration effect, to
attain the same equilibrium condition. But as we will argue
below, this course of affairs may have some extremely salutary side-effects on the general socioeconomic equilibrium
of the world as a whole.

We now turn to system-category III—that is, to the Soviet-type countries. In the base period A, we clearly have
here the category most out of equilibrium. Not only are
two of the three necessary conditions not satisfied, but the
degree of nonfulfillment of the two is considerable. Moreover, the "mixed" result under E:II is imputable solely to
distributional efficiency, which is quite high as a general
rule. Allocational efficiency, on the other hand, to which
we have been giving more emphasis throughout (because
it is generally inherent in a system and cannot be so easily

changed as can distributional efficiency) is quite unsatisfactory; it will be of considerable relevance in the analysis that follows.

Recalling again our simple theory of dynamic adjustment, we can conclude that the unsatisfactory initial conditions of the 1950's contain an enormous potential for change in the direction of equilibrium. And in fact, with just about one third of the time between periods A and B elapsed, a good deal of such change, in actuality or in the form of a blueprint, has been observable in many countries belonging to system-category III. Decentralization, markets, incentives, profit maximization—and even in some cases producers' codetermination—are all concepts which have increasingly entered the vocabulary of East European, including Russian, politicians and economists, and in some cases have reached the state of practical application.

In the best Marxist tradition, it can be said that the material sphere involving our necessary condition E:II has been the principal moving force of these actual and potential reforms. The nonfulfillment of the two self-determination conditions, save for outer political self-determination, has not substantially affected the thinking of the reformers. The principal vehicle of the reforms again is a crude demonstration effect: the relative (allocational) success of western market economies which operate on a profit incentive and competition, as compared with the low labor productivity and the slow growth and even stagnation in some instances of system-category III. Another pragmatic factor, less willingly acknowledged, is the success of "revisionist" system-category I in the sphere of economic efficiency.

We thus have, as the dominant dynamic force of category III in the period *A–B*, twofold emulation in the sphere of allocational efficiency, under the equilibrium condition E:II. Unfortunately for category III, the dominant force here seems to emulate category II, which leads at least temporarily to a second-best solution, with the more subtle virtues of self-determination and producer's democracy at first remaining neglected. We thus can make a tentative prediction for period *B*—and a more reliable one for period *C*—that system-category III (or at least the greater number of its members) will have equilibrium condition E:II fulfilled.[4]

That the same may happen with respect to E:I—that is, that economic self-determination may become the rule in period *B* for category III—can be conjectured, but with less probability attached to the expectation. We make the conjecture primarily on the grounds that (1) there exist some, even if only a few, experiments with economic self-determination at least in countries outside the Soviet Union, (2) it would be difficult for periods as long as two or three decades to have a workable profit-type incentive scheme in socialist enterprises without participation of the workers in management and income, and (3) governments which at least in part must in the long run concede to popular aspirations for democracy and self-determination, will at first find it easier to do so in the economic than in the political sphere. The last argument also indicates a negative predic-

---

[4] Note that the fulfillment of E:II is by and large consistent with the emulation of category II provided that the distributional efficiency realized at present in category III is retained. Of course, emulation of category I would be bound to lead to an even more perfect attainment of E:II.

tion in the political sphere for system III in period B. A fulfillment of P:I can only be expected in a later period, tentatively characterized here as period C; and the expectation would be much stronger if economic self-determination, that is, equilibrium condition E:I, were achieved in period B. We are again invoking here the consistency of human desires and aspirations, which, after an extensive and lasting experience with economic self-determination, should lead to political self-determination. In all that we have just said about system-category III, obviously, we have in mind a "central tendency" among the members of the category; extreme instances, such as Czechoslovakia on one end and China on the other, may undergo comparatively faster and slower transformations respectively, especially if they can attain and/or preserve outer political self-determination.

If it is difficult, in the case of categories I, II, and III, to foresee with any accuracy the dynamic process of transformation into an equilibrium state, it is virtually impossible to do so for category IV, which contains the rather heterogeneous group of developing countries. Instead of attempting any such predictions, we will rather formulate some possibilities that may be thought of as tentative recommendations to the less-advanced countries, or as "hopeful" expectations.

The state of disequilibrium of category IV in the base period is no less pronounced than that of category III. The latent forces of dynamic adjustment and the evolutionary potential thus are very strong in category IV (note that we are not speaking here of an economic growth potential, but rather of the potential for social systems to evolve toward equilibrium in the sense used in the study). However, the only prediction that we can make is that as a result of the dynamic potential, the equilibrium state will be reached at some point, perhaps a good deal later than our period C. The speed of adjustment will depend crucially on the degree to which the less-developed countries are able in their evolution to remain independent of the two major world system-prototypes, that is, our categories II and III.

Not only would imitation of either system-category II or III involve too roundabout an itinerary toward a final equilibrium, but a continuing dependence on either or both of the two prototypes is likely to continue a state of evolutionary paralysis. Indeed, the doctrinal foundations of categories II and III are so diametrically opposed that when entering simultaneously the sphere of category IV, they tend to neutralize each other like acids and alkalis, and thus lead to very little, if any, good effect. In this context, the decline during the 1960's of concern for and solidarity with the less-developed countries on the part of advanced countries, which constitutes a definite intermediate-run handicap for the less-developed nations, may turn out to be a significant advantage in the long run; that is, it may lead to a more direct path toward the fulfillment of all three equilibrium conditions—and thus shorten the process of adjustment by perhaps fifty years or more. The most tangible and perhaps most relevant implication of a more direct adjustment path would be a far earlier achievement of maximum economic efficiency. In the long run, the implied gain in efficiency may be well worth the aid that the less-developed countries might have received with system-oriented ties attached.

But the full benefit for the less-developed countries, in adopting a more direct way of progressing as fast as possible toward a full general equilibrium, is far more impor-

tant than the material gains just alluded to. The more direct
way also implies an early fulfillment of equilibrium condition E:I, which in practical terms means the direct and active involvement of large segments of the population in the
development process. This in turn involves education and
above all the development of human self-respect, and of
changing attitudes and outlooks, all of which are so important for the true social progress of a country.

Perhaps most important of all is the potential impact of
the "direct way" by category IV on the over-all balance
and distribution of respect among nations. As it stands, category IV is almost exclusively composed of countries that
are second-class world citizens economically and even politically. Moreover, in many respects the second-class position of the less-developed countries is tending to be accentuated rather than eliminated. In this general atmosphere,
the achievement of evolutional superiority by the nations
of category IV in the form of an earlier fulfillment of condition E:I and of the equilibrium in general would be extremely salutary. Indeed there would be nothing better
from the point of view of the equilibrium of human relations in the world than for those who today are powerful
and "superior" to be forced to learn something fundamentally good from those who today are poor and weak.

But I have already transgressed the limit of reasonably
reliable prediction or conjecture, and it is time to end this
part of our discussion. By way of a summary of the projected evolutionary pattern of the four system-categories,
see Figure 1. It is nothing but an extension of Table 1 (p.
80), which was designed to reflect the actual—or initial—
conditions in period *A*. A set of arrows leading from earlier to later periods for different system-categories and equi-

librium conditions is designed to recall some of the tentative causal or emulative relationships that we have suggested. Some others we have not included, but the reader may want to do so. For example, there is no doubt that the fulfillment of P:I, in system-category II—even if imperfect in the 1950's—has had and will have impact on developments in the political dimension of the other categories. We have not indicated such a relationship in our schema, however,

System-category:	I			II			III			IV		
Equilibrium condition:	P:I	E:I	E:II	P:I	E:I	E:II	P:I	E:I	E:II	P:I	E:I	E:II
Period: A	±	+	±	±	−	±	−	−	±	±	−	±
B	+	±	+	+	−	+	−	+	+	(±)	(+)	(±)
C	+	+	+	+	+	+	+	+	+	(+)	(+)	(+)

Figure 1. Schematic representation of the future evolution of principal system-categories

because (apart from not wanting to crowd the diagram) it seems to me that in all the other categories, *true* political self-determination must come as an aftereffect and logical extension of economic self-determination, often only in conjunction with the attainment of full equilibrium in the second economic condition. All "predictions" for system-category IV are bracketed to indicate their conditional and very tentative nature. In fact, question marks might be preferable in this connection.

A Postscript on Convergence ≺≺≺≺≺≺

We have now come to the conclusion of our argument; there remains, however, one related matter which we ought not to neglect. It is the possible future convergence of the major social systems in the world today. Although it was not our principal purpose, a good part of the discussion we have presented here can be conceived of, or viewed, as a theory of convergence. Thereby we enter into a question which has excited recent interest among political economists. Insofar as we foresee and aspire to convergence toward a future equilibrium state, we stand with such writers as Tinbergen, Galbraith, and (more recently) Wiles, and take issue with such others as Brzezinski and Wiles earlier.[1] At the same time, it turns out that we have some-

[1] Jan Tinbergen, "Do Communist and Free Economies Show a Converging Pattern?" *Soviet Studies*, XII (April 1961), 334–341; Tinbergen, H. Linnemann, and J. P. Pronk, *Convergence of Economic Systems in East and West* (Rotterdam, 1965); John Kenneth Galbraith, *The New Industrial State* (Boston, 1967); P. J. D. Wiles, "Fifty Years After: What Future for Communism?" *Lloyds Bank Review*, No. 86 (October, 1967), pp. 36–48; Zbigiew Brzezinski and Samuel P. Huntington, *Political Power: USA/USSR* (New York, 1964); Wiles, "Will Capitalism and Communism Spontaneously Converge?" *Encounter*, XX (June 1963), 84–90.

thing in common with certain of the "divergence" theories, and tend not to agree entirely with some of the points made to substantiate convergence.

The convergence theories themselves, let it be noted, are widely divergent in nature. For example, the most complete is Professor Tinbergen's almost taxonomic enumeration of the specific aspects of convergence.[2] Galbraith, not attempting an overarching theory but limiting himself to a more confined subject matter, emphasizes the fundamental similarity between modern large firms in East and West. Within an area more specific yet, Pryor emphasizes the share of government spending among the major world powers.[3]

In opposition stand those who see the basic tendency among major societies as divergence. Brzezinski, for example, finds the powers to be evolving independently of one another, and doubts that they are converging.[4] We might agree with the notion of independent evolution, but in our view the evolutionary forces, in the very long run at least, are the same. Wiles believed that Yugoslavia will converge less, not more than others.[5] Remembering our evaluation of Yugoslavia's fulfillment of the several equilibrium conditions, the reader will realize that we are in agreement with this viewpoint too. Since Yugoslavia, by our measure, is nearer than other countries today to an equilibrium situation, it will have less distance to travel to equilibrium; in that sense, it will "converge" less.

[2] Tinbergen, *Soviet Studies*, pp. 334–341.
[3] Frederic L. Pryor, *Public Expenditures in Communist and Capitalist Nations* (London, 1968).
[4] Brzezinski, *op. cit.*
[5] Wiles, *Lloyds Bank Review*, p. 48.

Finally, a comment on two of Tinbergen's key ideas. In his view, the abandonment by the Soviet Union of an attempt at labor management marked a turn toward the West, therefore in the direction of convergence.[6] In the narrow sense, this is correct, in that the structure of the firm in the two systems became more nearly similar. But in our mind, workers' management was abrogated as a result of a disequilibrium situation in the political plane.[7] In terms of the long-range equilibrium we have projected, both the Soviet and the capitalist systems have yet to travel to an equilibrium state. In this context, the episode described by Tinbergen classifies as a divergence from a state closer to equilibrium to one less close.

With another of Tinbergen's ideas we stand in wholehearted agreement, and on this note we may conclude our study. He advocates the skipping of stages by the developing countries on their road of advancement.[8] We have endorsed the same. We have also expressed the hope that the less-developed countries, by moving more directly toward a state of socioeconomic equilibrium, can in the long run lead the way for the currently advanced nations which are committed without exception to one or the other major world system. By so doing they would help to establish in the world a better balance of respect among nations.

[6] *Soviet Studies*, p. 333.

[7] As we have argued in Chapter 7 in terms of our general equilibrium analysis, a disequilibrium in one dimension causes disequilibrium—or prevents equilibrium—in another.

[8] Tinbergen, *Soviet Studies*, p. 341.

Index ≺≺≺≺≺≺≺≺≺≺≺≺≺≺≺

The Participatory Economy

Designed by Randy H. Marsh.
Composed by Vail-Ballou Press, Inc.,
in 11 point linotype Janson, 3 points leaded,
with display lines in Corvinus Light with Weiss Border no. 4226.
Printed letterpress from type by Vail-Ballou Press
on Warren's No. 66 antique text, 60 pound basis,
with the Cornell University Press watermark.
Bound by Vail-Ballou Press
in Interlaken Pallium book cloth
and stamped in imitation gold foil.